THY KINGDOM COME

A Biblical Introduction to the Bahá'í Faith

THE SEVEN VIALS OF WRATH
poured out upon the earth. (*Revelation 16:1-7*)

THY KINGDOM COME

A Biblical Introduction to the Bahá'í Faith

by
Thomas Tai-Seale

KALIMÁT PRESS
LOS ANGELES

Manufactured in the United States of America.

Library of Congress Cataloguing in Publication Data

Tai-Seale, Thomas.
Thy kingdom come : a biblical introduction to the Bahá'í faith / by Thomas Tai-Seale.
p. cm.
Includes bibliographical references.
ISBN 0-933770-93-6
1. Bible—Prophecies—Baha'i Faith.
2. Baha'i Faith—Doctrines. I. Title.
BS649.B33T35 1992
220.1'5—dc20 93-6484
CIP

To those Bahá'ís gone before me whose good character
has embraced me and led me toward truth.

AUTHOR'S NOTE

This book has been over twelve years in the making. But it would never have been begun at all were it not for the example set by a few exceptional people whom I met as I was becoming a Bahá'í. I am thinking particularly of Gertrude Gilam; Stanwood Cobb; Thomas, Martin, and William Varner, and their wives (especially Margaret, who I knew the best); Behrooz Rouhani; Carey and Murph Murphy; Gary, and later, Jeanne McDaniel; Benjamin and Francine Levy; Bob and Marion Hatch; Carol and Larry Miller; Jane Failey; Randy and Sharon Wright; Carl Swanson; Klaus and Arefeh Langkilde; Thomas Grant (now Asada-Grant); Lilian Garnet; Doris Ebbert; and Olga Finke. There were many others in my early days, but these people were the first through whom my faith grew. I must also mention two Hands of the Cause of God whose examples were critical in developing my faith: Dhikru'lláh Khadem and William Sears.

When I began this book I was living alone in a small, one-room house on a farm (part of the University of Bophuthatswana) in Southern Africa. I was teaching science to the agriculture students of the university, and my days were very full. My habit was to read and study biblical and Bahá'í commentary every workday evening from 5:00 p.m. till midnight. On weekends, I continued working on my biblical studies—often for eighteen hours a day. This went on for the better part of five years and continues still to some degree. The majestic African countryside provided an ideal environment for reflection. It was wonderful to be free of telephones and televisions for years.

The price of such a schedule was high, however. I was often overworked, sometimes sick, and generally starved for intellectual and spiritual companionship. There could be no better friend in this regard than Hugh Baughan. When he came to work at the university and became my apartmentmate, he also became my chief advisor, confidant, and best friend. He is the most patient, principled, disciplined, and joyful man I have ever known. My sincere thanks also goes to Soheil Rawhani, whose visits to Taung (my place in Southern Africa) brought us infinite delight. Also, I must thank the gracious, pure-hearted Bahá'ís of Taung; especially Rre Moetapele; Dora, Isaac, and Panche Motlhale; Buddy Oliphant; Josiah; Rre Sams and Amelia.

The early versions of this manuscript were edited by one of the brightest women I have ever known: Thea Van Zijl. I am thrilled to say that since that time she has entered the Most Great Cause and became a Bahá'í. Latter versions of the manuscript were edited by Anthony Lee and Sherri Spicklemire. I am grateful for their skilled assistance.

I must also mention a few Bahá'ís in South Africa who helped me. Martin Konstant has been a wonderful correspondent and friend. At least one of his thoughts on the Bible has found its way onto these pages. Michelle and Alan Moore, Judy and Steve Worth, Wright Lechonchobe, Ephens and Nettie Senne, Ethel Motilenvane, Stanlake Kukama, Susie and Roy Simmerly, the Rawhanis, the Eshragis, and Lowell Johnson have all added immeasurably to my life and helped make this book possible through the force of their sustained love. There are others, too, whom I would like to mention if only my memory would serve me better. Surely they will know they have each played a part.

My eternal thanks go also and always to my helpmate in life, Ming, who since our meeting, has become my sun and moon, and to our little baby daughter, Sahar, about whose dawn we are all excited.

Tom Tai-Seale
Los Angeles, 1993

CONTENTS

A THRONE SET IN HEAVEN
and the twenty-four elders. (*Revelation 4:1-9*)

PREFACE

Although I was raised in a Christian home, my early biblical education was not very good. I was more often told what to believe than encouraged to struggle to discover meaning. I was especially baffled by biblical prophecies. They seemed so far-fetched that I could find little reason to think that they had anything to do with my life. Except to instill the fear that when the Lord came I might be left behind, the prophecies had no meaning for me.

The Bahá'í Faith has changed all that.[1] Bible prophecies now have tremendous and immediate meaning. This is because I have finally been challenged to look closely at what was written in scripture. What I have discovered in this review lies far beyond the limitations of my earlier biblical education.

This book is a rethinking of prophecy occasioned by

1. Diacritical marks are used for Arabic derived words throughout the text. It is best to learn a few vowels now. The á is pronounced like the "a" in "father." An unaccented a in an Arabic word is pronounced like the "a" in "man." The í is pronounced like "ee" in "beet." An unaccented i is pronounced like the "e" in "bet." Later we will see ú, which is pronounced as "oo" in "boot." The unaccented u is pronounced like "o" in "fort."

my contact with the Bahá'í Faith. It is also a history of events that are of supreme religious significance. And it is a profoundly Christian statement. I believe passionately in the divinity of Jesus, in the truth of His ministry, in the eternity of His message, and in the holiness of the Bible. It is the Bible which has been my touchstone of truth. Consequently, I have used primarily Christian texts for my proofs. Bahá'í texts are used as interpretive guides, but those references are most often placed in the footnotes. Except where noted, all Bible quotations are from the King James Version.[2]

The Christian reader will be challenged by this book. Interpretations will be put forth which can only be made by one who stands on the other side of a new faith. I write as a Christian who has found my heart's desire in the Bahá'í Faith; that is, as a Bahá'í of Christian background. I do not count myself a biblical scholar. I do not speak ancient languages, nor is Bible study my career. In this sense I am an average man. But the Bible is for average people and, as we all know, having a professional education in the Bible is no guarantee of being able to interpret it correctly. Each of us must wrestle independently with the scriptures of our faith so that the meaning we derive may truly be our own.

My aid to interpretation comes from reading many different Christian interpretations of scripture and from

2. The Scofield Reference Bible, New York, Oxford University Press, 1967, is most often used. This edition uses italics to indicate added or changed words. I have not indicated added or changed words in this text.

the Bahá'í writings. The diversity of Christian thought about prophecy is actually quite broad—broader than many Christians realize. Much of it is consistent with Bahá'í interpretation. This breadth of reading has been of inestimable aid to me. We should never be afraid to read and think.

I ask readers to suspend, for a moment, what they think they know about the meaning of prophecy. Read fully, unfettered by any previous ideas, what is presented here. And, at the end, make a decision. In reading, however, it is important to keep in mind that more than one interpretation of prophecy is not only possible but essential.[3] Thus, what follows is necessarily a partial interpretation of prophecy. Further, what follows is not a complete survey of biblical references to the Bahá'í Faith. As Shoghi Effendi, the Guardian of the Bahá'í Faith, makes plain:

> To attempt an exhaustive survey of the prophetic references to Bahá'u'lláh's Revelation would indeed be an impossible task. To this Bahá'u'lláh Himself bears witness: "All the Divine Books and Scriptures have predicted and announced unto men the advent of the Most Great Revelation. None can adequately recount the verses recorded in the Books of former

3. Bahá'u'lláh writes, "Know assuredly that just as thou firmly believest that the Word of God, exalted be His glory, endureth forever, thou must likewise, believe with undoubting faith that its meanings can never be exhausted" (*Gleanings from the Writings of Bahá'u'lláh*, Wilmette, Il: Bahá'í Publishing Trust, 1939) p. 175.

ages which forecast this supreme Bounty, this most mighty Bestowal."[4]

Nor is this meant to be a technical discourse, which is not useful in an introduction. In this interpretation of biblical prophecies, I have put forth my views simply to help make the work more readable. Unless otherwise noted, the reader should assume the interpretations are my own. That is, these are the interpretations of a single Bahá'í.

The Bahá'í Faith, of course, offers much more than biblical commentary and it is not necessary to embrace this Faith through its Bible interpretations. As with any religion, it is contact with the Author of the Faith and His words that is the primary basis for belief.

Beyond this contact, the best proof of a religion is the response it receives over time. Does the faith endure early challenges and grow? Does it produce saints and heroes? The proof of Christianity rests more upon the reality of Jesus, the truth of His words, and the response of His followers than on any Old Testament prophecies. Scriptural proofs may be a part of faith, but they are not a substitute for transforming contact with its Author. Still, the magnitude of the claim of the Bahá'ís, and the fact that they claim prophetic *fulfillment*, should command the attention of any Christian.

Finally, this book explains my belief that there have been three divine calls made to us since the time of Christ. Biblical prophecy is largely the story of these three advents.

4. Shoghi Effendi, *God Passes By* (Wilmette, Il: Bahá'í Publishing Trust, 1970) p. 100.

THY KINGDOM COME

A Biblical Introduction to the Bahá'í Faith

THE SECOND COMING
An artist's conception. (*Matthew 25:31-46*)

Chapter 1

HOW THE LORD WILL COME

I'm not sure whether I first heard it at Sunday school or in confirmation class, or whether I merely absorbed it from the prevailing Christian culture of the southern United States, where I grew up. But at some point it was impressed upon me that the Lord would return upon a cloud, and that when He returned the faithful would be gathered up to Him in the air. This, I was taught, was the literal truth. Armed with a belief such as this all other questions about the return of Christ were simply unimportant. What was important was to remain faithful to Jesus, so that when the Lord returned I would be counted among the believers.

The trouble with such a view is that it seriously misrepresents the history of prophetic interpretation, even within the greater Christian tradition. This literal view is, after all, only an interpretation, and only one of the many which are possible. We have good reason to consider other views. If the literal view is wrong, then we have not only been guilty of uncritically accepting a very fanciful construct, we may also be culpable for the consequences of our misbelief.

In this chapter I will look at important scriptures that speak of the coming of the Lord and I will present some of the traditional interpretations—as I was taught them. Then, I will review these views in the light of broader Christian thought and the interpretations presented in the Bahá'í Faith.

Wars, Famines, Disease, and Earthquakes Will Precede Him

Over time, the notion has developed among Christians that wars, famines, disease, and earthquakes will immediately precede the coming of the Lord. On close examination, however, we find this is not what the scriptures say. A representative verse reads:

> And ye shall hear of wars and rumors of wars; see that ye be not troubled; for all these things must come to pass, but the end is not yet. For nation shall rise against nation, and kingdom against kingdom; and there shall be famines, and pestilence, and earthquakes, in various places. And all these are the beginning of sorrows. *Matthew 24:6-8.*

Nowhere in these verses do we read that the tragic events will *immediately* precede the advent of the Lord. Rather, we are told that these naturally occurring events will continue to happen—even as they always have—until the coming of the Lord and beyond. Wars, famines, epidemic diseases, and earthquakes are regular and periodic events. The point of the passage seems to be that a long time will pass before the coming of the Lord and that these tragic events will not end with His coming. Indeed, these events are but the beginnings of sorrows. The sorrows may actually get worse *after* the advent of the Lord.

Of course, the verses also may have symbolic meaning. As long as our theology, our religious organizations, and the regulation of our society are not built upon divine principles, we will be subject to the *wars* of reformers, the *famines* of faith,[1] the *pestilence* of corruption, and the *earthquakes* of spiritual upheaval. We are not promised that this instability will stop when the True One appears. Indeed, it may worsen because of His appearance and our consequent reaction.

He Will Come in the Clouds

Jesus, we have been taught, will come in the clouds. This is what a representative verse says:

> And then shall appear the sign of the Son of man in heaven; and then shall all the tribes of the earth mourn, and they shall see the Son of man coming in the *clouds of heaven* with power and great glory. *Matthew 24:30* (Emphasis mine.)

1. The possibility of a symbolic interpretation to these words

But are the clouds of heaven the same as the clouds of earth? Did Christ mean for us to believe that He will come riding on the physical clouds that encircle our planet? Our answer begins to unfold as we ponder the questions that arise from a literal interpretation. Will the Lord have to ride around the entire planet on clouds for all to see Him? If He rides *in* the clouds, as the verse says, will we be able to see Him? Will our Messiah have weight if He rides the clouds; that is, will He be a physical being? Or will the clouds have to be specially formed to be able to support Him?

These questions expose the absurdity of the literal interpretation. Perhaps, then, the clouds of heaven are not the physical clouds of earth. In fact, the purpose of the cloud analogy is to suggest the nature of the spiritual event. Physical clouds have many properties: they give rain and shade; they can be foreboding and terrifying or graceful and lofty; they move by a will that is not ours; and they can obscure the sun as well as reflect its light. The clouds of heaven may do these things as well, but the action would occur in our souls.

Consider, also, the Old Testament use of the word "cloud." There it seems to symbolize the boundaries of our knowledge. For example, the Lord came in a thick cloud to Moses whose knowledge of the Lord was,

---

is shown by Old Testament passages such as this: "Behold the days come, saith the Lord God, that I will send a famine in the land, not a famine of bread, nor a thirst for water, but of hearing the words of the Lord. And they shall wander from sea to sea, and from the north even to the east; they shall run to and fro to seek the word of the Lord, and shall not find it." *Amos 8:11-12*

therefore, limited.[2] But the knowledge of the followers of Moses was even more limited. Not only could they not know the Lord directly—this was Moses' prerogative—they could not even know the work Moses did on the mountain with the Lord.[3] Both Moses and the Lord were obscured by the clouds upon Mount Sinai.[4] It is significant, then, that we are promised that the Lord will come in clouds. Again, it underscores the limitations of our knowledge of what happens when God speaks to man.

The image of the Lord coming in the clouds also says to us that He will bring the life-giving spiritual rain and shade of new teachings; that He will provide warnings of storms to come if we do not turn to Him and respond to His Word; that He will move by a power far beyond our control; and that His coming may be obscured by the clouds of our own imagination. The point is that in each of these interpretations it requires insight, not

2. "And the Lord said unto Moses, Lo, I come unto thee in a thick cloud, that the people may hear when I speak with thee, and believe thee forever." *Exodus 19:9*

3. "And ye [Moses] came near and stood under the mountain; and the mountain burned with fire unto the midst of heaven, with darkness, clouds, and thick darkness. And the Lord spoke unto you out of the midst of the fire. Ye heard the voice of the words but saw no similitude; only ye heard a voice. And he declared unto you his covenant, which he commanded you to perform, even ten commandments; and he wrote them upon two tablets of stone." *Deuteronomy 4:11-13*

4. "And Moses went up into the mount, and a cloud covered the mount. And the Glory of the Lord abode upon Mount Sinai, and the cloud covered it six days; and the seventh day he called unto Moses out of the midst of the cloud." *Exodus 24:15-16*

sight, to see the coming of the Promised One. Indeed, it is clear that it would be quite possible to miss the coming of the Lord in the clouds of heaven, because to find Him we would have to develop spiritual, not physical, vision. These interpretations are consistent with Bahá'í Writings about the meaning of "clouds" in prophecy.[5]

He Will Descend from Heaven

We also have been taught that Jesus will descend from heaven. The verses about Jesus' departure and return to earth read,

> And when he [Jesus] had spoken these things, while they beheld, he was taken up, and a cloud received him out of sight. And while they looked steadfastly toward heaven as he went up, behold, two men stood by them in white apparel; Who also said, Ye men of Galilee, why stand ye gazing up into heaven? This same Jesus, who is taken up from heaven, shall so come in like manner as ye have seen him go into heaven. *Acts 1:9-11*

5. Clouds are a recurring symbol in the Bible and in the Bahá'í writings, occurring hundreds of times and used in many ways. Bahá'u'lláh interprets the clouds in the verses of Matthew above in two ways. He writes: "They [the Chosen Ones of God] are sent

Many of us have been taught to interpret these verses to mean that Jesus physically went up into the sky, and that He will return in the same way. But was Jesus taken up into the sky physically, or, was He taken up into the spiritual heavens?

Again, literal interpretations for this sort of passage are very weak. Consider, if all objects in the verse: Jesus, His Return, heaven, and the cloud are interpreted as being real physical objects, then the resulting interpretation is inconsistent with what we know of physical objects. Real clouds can't support weight and people have a hard time breathing in the distant skies (heaven). If it was the physical body of Jesus that was taken up into the sky, where did it go? Where is it now? If we concede that not all objects in the verse are meant to be interpreted literally, then we admit that the verse must be interpreted, in part at least, symbolically.

Beyond this, it is important to note that this fantastic story is not recorded anywhere else in scripture. If the event had occurred physically, if Jesus had been

---

forth through the transcendent power of the Ancient of Days, and are raised up by the exalted will of God, the most mighty King. This is what is meant by the words: 'coming in the clouds of heaven' "— *The Kitáb-i-Iqán*: *The Book of Certitude* (Wilmette, Il.: Bahá'í Publishing Trust, 1931) p. 67. He also explains that clouds symbolize " 'those things that are contrary to the ways and desires of men' such as the annulment of laws of a former Dispensation, or the appearance of the Promised One in the image of mortal man 'with such human limitations as eating, drinking, poverty and riches, glory and abasement, sleeping and waking, and such other things as cast doubt in the minds of men.' " *The Kitáb-i-Iqán*, pp. 71-74.

taken up physically into the skies, it would certainly have been mentioned in the gospels. If we are fair, we must suspect that this verse is a myth that has been told about Jesus. If, then, it is to have any meaning, we are forced to interpret it symbolically, where it may again become rich in meaning.

But even from scripture we should know not to interpret this passage literally. We all know that Jesus did not come to earth from the physical sky. Rather, He was born of a woman. Therefore, when He said, "For I came down from heaven, not to do mine own will but the will of him that sent me," no one thinks He was talking about having descended to earth from the skies.[6] Then why do we insist that Jesus left and must return to earth via the literal heavens? When Jesus said, "And no man hath ascended up to heaven, but he that came down from heaven, even the Son of man who is in heaven," we must interpret the ascending to heaven in the same way that we understand the coming down from heaven: that is, in a symbolic way.[7] Thus we have been promised that Christ will return from the heaven of the realm of God, not that He will descend from the sky.

The Dead Will Rise to Meet Him

We have been taught that the dead in Christ will rise first at His coming. The verses read,

6. *John 6:38.*
7. *John 3:13.*

> For the Lord himself shall descend from heaven with a shout, with the voice of the archangel, and with the trump of God; and the dead in Christ shall rise first. *1 Thessalonians 4:16.*

Does this mean that Christian bones in the tombs will regather flesh and arise out of graves? Is there, then, a still vital connection between these bones and dust and the soul? Have not these steadfast souls met their Lord already? And if the souls of the departed return to earth, will they return through the grave from which they departed? How will these reconstituted physical beings walk on the air? And where in the air will they go? How far out? What will they do there? Will they need oxygen? Will they, in fact, be physical beings? Will we be able to see them?

Let us consider less fantastic meanings. What if "the dead in Christ" refers to the faithful souls of departed Christians who, from their much better other-worldly perspective, will be able to see the Lord's advent first.[8] What then will the rest of us be doing when He comes? Probably the same thing we've always been doing: eat-

8. The forerunner of the Bahá'í Faith, the Báb, proclaimed to His first disciples, "Lo thy Lord God is come, and with Him is the company of His angels arrayed before Him." *The Dawnbreakers* (Wilmette, Il.: Bahá'í Publishing Trust, 1932) p. 93. At this early time in His ministry, the Báb had few followers. The company of angels, then, that were arrayed before Him must have been in heaven, not on earth. The arrayed angels must have been com-

ing, drinking, sleeping, working, and playing.[9] Thus it would be the dead in Christ who see Him first. The living may not see Him. Why? Because His advent may not be fantastic in an earthly sense, and because our consideration of His cause is likely to be hampered by the clouds of our deficient understanding, arrogance, and imagination.

He Will Come with Angels

And what of the angels that are supposed to accompany the Lord? The verse reads,

> And he shall send his *angels* with a great sound of a trumpet, and they shall gather together his elect from the four winds, from one end of heaven to the other. *Matthew 24:31* (Emphasis mine.)

posed of the souls of the faithful from previous religious dispensations.

Another interpretation is also possible and legitimate. As the new religion grows, there will be established new saints on earth, and these new believers are called from a condition of death to one of life. The dead are raised again. This second interpretation is also found in Bahá'í writings. For example, Bahá'u'lláh writes, "Well is it with the slumberer who is stirred by the Breeze of God and ariseth from amongst the dead, directing his steps toward the Way of the Lord." *Tablets of Bahá'u'lláh* (Haifa: Bahá'í World Center, 1978) p. 13.

9. The wording here is suggested by *Matthew 24:37-39*. See p. 18, below.

The word "angel" may be better understood as "saint," as it is used in Paul's letters to the Thessalonians.[10] Maybe, then, the angels are the *new* believers themselves, those who recognize the Promised One when He comes. But if this is so, then we have not been promised a visible fantastic thing. Saints are hard to recognize. Would we recognize a Peter or a Paul if we saw him in our day? Would we quarrel with him if his message was new? And what if we met a believer who had not the faith of Peter, or the eloquence of Paul? Would we be able to see an angel doing God's redemptive work in whatever measure?

Alternatively, consider that the angels we have been promised are indeed those of the spiritual world. We may never catch sight of them. Rather, we may only feel their influence when we arise to do God's work. Consider this: In any spiritual teaching encounter between two people, there are actually three components: the two individuals and the wondrous influence of the Holy Spirit, the angelic force that wafts upon us, granting understanding and confirmation. But feeling this force is entirely conditional upon our own efforts at teaching. It has nothing to do with visible angels. What is being proclaimed here is that we may not know the angels have come until we ourselves rise up and take a

10. "To the end he may establish your hearts unblamable in holiness before God, even our Father, at the coming of our Lord Jesus Christ with all his saints." *1 Thessalonians 3:13*. "When he shall come to be glorified in his saints, and to be admired in all them that believe (because our testimony among you was believed) in that day." *2 Thessalonians 1:10*

step of faith in proclaiming the Lord's cause. Only then will we experience the angelic force of the kingdom and know that the angels have come.

Both of these interpretations are found in the Bahá'í writings, and both stress that careful discernment is required to "see" the angels of the Lord.[11]

All Eyes Will See Him

Another thing we have been taught is that:

> Behold he cometh with clouds, and every eye shall see him, and they also who pierced him; and all the kindreds of the earth shall wail because of him. *Revelation 1:7*

Many have interpreted this to mean that Jesus's coming will be dramatic and upon the physical clouds. But could these clouds be symbols, as we've already discussed? Could the author of the Book of Revelation be

11. Bahá'u'lláh writes, "By 'angels' is meant those who, reinforced by the power of the spirit, have consumed, with the fire of the love of God, all human traits and limitations, and have clothed themselves with the attributes of the most exalted Beings and of the Cherubim." *The Kitáb-i-Iqán*, p. 78.

The other interpretation is found in writings such as these: "Verily, We behold you from Our realm of glory, and shall aid whosoever will arise for the triumph of Our Cause with the hosts of the Concourse on high and a company of our favored angels." *Gleanings from the Writings of Bahá'u'lláh*, p. 139.

warning that our vision of Jesus's coming may be obscured by our lack of insight? Yes, He will come in a way for all to see, that is, He will reveal His cause openly. But will every eye that "sees" Him recognize that this is the Lord upon the clouds of the Kingdom?

Consider now those who pierced Jesus. They have literally been dead almost two thousand years. How will they see Him when He comes? Perhaps those who pierced Him will see Him coming—that is, recognize His spiritual ascendancy or His return—from the life after death, in the spiritual world. Alternatively, some have suggested that "those that pierced Him" refer more broadly to the Romans and Jews. But are the Romans and Jews of today the same as those of antiquity? Are they those that pierced him? No. Thus, the Romans and Jews who rejected Him would have to see His coming from the next world. So, "those that pierced Him" might refer to those who have died long ago and therefore would have to see His coming from the world beyond.

Finally, those that pierced him could refer to people who are alive at His coming. If this is the case, they would have to represent or act like those that originally pierced Him. They would not, however, have to be Romans or Jews. Consider that those who oppose a prophet of God in one age and those who oppose a prophet of God in another age are functionally and spiritually identical. The prophecy that those who pierced Jesus will see Him coming with clouds may refer to a persecution that will occur at His return. We are being told He may be pierced again; He may suffer again at our hands. But His advent upon the clouds, moving by God's will, indicates that He will not be stopped by our actions. Either in this world or in the one beyond, the persecutors of the returned Christ will be made to recognize the error of their ways. As we shall see, this same image of the Lord being pierced and caught up on clouds where His enemies behold Him is used later in the Book of Revelation in reference to the two prophet witnesses in Chapter 11, verse 12. When we review this chapter, it will become clear that the verses above have nothing to do with literal clouds.

He Will Come Suddenly

Many of us have been taught that the Lord's return will happen suddenly; that He will catch us unaware like a thief in the night. The prophecy of the Lord's return like a thief is one of the most persistent prophetic themes in the New Testament.[12] One version of it is printed below:

> Watch, therefore; for ye know not what hour your Lord doth come. But know this, that if the householder had known in what watch the thief would come, he would have watched, and would not allowed his house to be broken into. *Matthew 24:42-43*

12. It occurs in *2 Peter 3:10; Revelation 3:3; Matthew 24:42-44; Mark 13:33-37; and Luke 12:38.*

There is another interpretation to consider.[13] A thief in the night is silent. He steals into a house, takes what he wants, and leaves. The occupants of the house don't know the thief is there unless they awaken. They may even dream that they are awake. But unless they actually catch the thief, they are proven to be asleep in spiritual reality.

Every entrance happens suddenly. The parable, however, is far more than a claim that the Lord's advent will occur suddenly, or a warning that we may be judged abruptly. It is a testament to the fact that we may be judged and not know it. This unawareness of the judgment is what being asleep means. And the Lord, in the prophecy, comes to those who are asleep. We are being told that most of us will be unaware of the Lord's return, even though our sleep may be filled with hopes and dreams of His arrival.

The prophecy also tells us that it is only the returned Lord who determines who is awake and who is sleeping. Thus, the Message that we will all eventually awaken to is not that the Lord is coming, but that He has already been here. If we hear other voices in the night, other stories about how it will be when He returns, these are but other sleepers dreaming. The voice worth listening to is the one that can speak of the Lord's actual return. If we wish to catch the thief we must not be afraid to open our eyes. He may already have come.

13. Bahá'í writings suggest this interpretation. For example, see 'Abdu'l-Bahá, *Selections from the Writings of 'Abdu'l-Bahá*, (Haifa: Bahá'í World Center, 1978) p. 35 and 199.

Everything Will Be Made Perfect When He Comes

Most of us have been taught that when the Promised One comes everything will be made perfect for the believers and, of course, we all think of ourselves as believers.[14] But a fuller look at scripture gives us another view. The New Testament's mention of Noah is instructive. The verses read,

> But as the days of Noah were, so shall also the coming of the Son of man be. For as in the days that were before the flood they were eating and drinking, marrying, and giving in marriage, until the day that Noah entered the ark, And knew not until the flood came, and took them all away, so shall also the coming of the Son of man be. *Matthew 24:37-39*

Did Noah find many believers to take with him in the Ark? No. Noah found a population that was not interested in his warnings. Those who believe that the Lord's advent will be preceded by great disasters obvious to all must ask themselves: Did Noah come before or after the flood? Could it be that the Promised One

14. This belief is anchored in *Revelation 21:5* which states, "Behold, I make all things new." However, this statement comes after the Promised One comes and is made to do battle with the kings of the earth. In no sense can it be considered an instant fixing of all our problems immediately upon the advent of the Lord.

will come, issue many warnings, find people disbelieving, suffer as a consequence of our disbelief, and build an ark of a new Faith all before the rains come? This is what Bahá'ís believe has happened. It has been raining for some time now. Is it time to look for the ark? If we don't, we may find ourselves still wondering about the return of Christ as we take our last breaths.

The Stars Will Fall

Yet another thing we have been taught is that fantastic physical signs will accompany the return of the Lord. The verse which engenders this belief reads:

> Immediately after the tribulation of those days shall the sun be darkened, and the moon shall not give its light, and the stars shall fall from heaven, and the powers of the earth shall be shaken. *Matthew 24:29*

But this prophecy is in symbolic form, as the Bible itself clearly reveals. In the Bible rulers are suns, chief ministers are moons, and lesser leaders are stars. This applies to the lights of both secular and religious realms. In the Old Testament the pharaoh is a light that God threatens to extinguish.[15] The king of Babylon was condemned by God because he tried to ascend like a sun

15. *Ezekiel 32.*

into heaven above the heights of the clouds.[16] Thus, God promised to pull the stars of the heaven of Babylon down and to darken the sun and moon of the kingdom. This darkening of the lights of leaders did not happen in an instant, but gradually, over a period of time. And it is likely that those who were spiritually condemned were not even aware of the judgment made against them or of its connection to any action of theirs against God. Have the lights of our society grown dim? Are we aware of any act of omission or commission which may have been the cause of our slow demise?

Jesus, too, was a sun. He said, "I am the light of the world," and the clergy of both Old and New Testaments are proclaimed to be like stars.[17] The Bible promises us a day in which the brilliant coming of the Lord will obviate the need for any other light.[18] The stars will fall and a new heaven will be rolled out. While Christ is a light that can never die, Christ's ministry must eventually be seen as a day in the week of the Lord. For if the return of Christ is to have any meaning, it too must be a day. Being faithful to the Lord thus means that as the new day dawns, we must recognize its light as the promised light and understand that the old form of Christianity must give way to the new.

16. *Isaiah 13-14.*

17. *John 8:12.* Also see *Daniel 12:3* and *Jude 1:12* for biblical references to leaders being like stars.

18. *Revelation 21:23* reads, "And the city [the New Jerusalem] *had no need of the sun, neither of the moon*, to shine in it; for the glory of God did light it, and the Lamb is the lamp of it." (Emphasis mine.)

Wheat and Tares Will Be Separated

Perhaps a more basic reason that we don't want to consider that our religious lights may be dimmed is that many of us, like the Jews in Christ's time, have become complacent and arrogant in our religion. But is our religion that which Christ promised? Before the Kingdom can be established on earth, a reckoning must occur. That reckoning may be against nonbelievers, but it is not for us to decide who they are. And even among the believers, we are told, there are many tares mixed in with the wheat.[19] There are too many warring theologies, too many interpretations, too many different churches. Faith still may be simple, but finding the right spiritual home is now enormously complex. We have been promised a sorting. Is it happening now? Will we be happy when it does happen?

There Will Be False Prophets

Finally, we have been taught that false prophets will come. One set of verses reads:

> And Jesus answered and said unto them, Take heed that no one deceive you. For many shall come in my name, saying, I am Christ; and shall deceive many. *Matthew 24:4-5*

19. *Matthew 13:24.*

The New Testament itself, before it closed, introduced us to several false prophets who were operating in the first century after Jesus's crucifixion. There was Theudas, who "boasted himself to be somebody," and Judas of Galilee, who "drew away many people after him."[20] There was Simon, who "in the same city [as Philip taught] used sorcery and bewitched the people of Samaria, giving out that he was some great one."[21] There was also "that Egyptian, who before these days madest an uproar, and leddest out into the wilderness four thousand men that were murderers."[22] The Book of Revelation introduced us to the Nicolaitans,[23] the followers of Balaam,[24] and the prophetess Jezebel.[25] In fact, there were many false prophets in early Christianity.[26]

20. *Acts 5:34-6.*

21. *Acts 8:9-10.*

22. *Acts 21:38.* Josephus said the army of "this Egyptian" was 30,000 strong.

23. *Revelation 2:6 and 15.*

24. *Revelation 2:14.*

25. *Revelation 2:20.*

26. Eusebius, the first great church historian, quotes from Hegesippus (100-180 A.D.): "When James the Righteous had suffered martyrdom like the Lord and for the same reasons, Symeon the son of his uncle Clopas, was appointed bishop. He being cousin of the Lord, it was the universal demand that he should be second. They used to call the Church a virgin for this reason, that she had not been seduced by listening to nonsense. But Thebuthis, because he had not been made bishop, began to seduce her by means of the seven sects (to which he himself belonged) among the people. From these came Simon and his Simonians,

In our own day the formation of new churchs around charismatic leaders is commonplace in both the East and the West. Furthermore, most of us certainly have had cause to wonder if some of those claiming to be inspired leaders are in reality false prophets. Apparently, there will always be false prophets. But is the existence of these false prophets sufficient reason to close our ears to all voices? Operating on this principle, the voice of Jesus would never have been heard. Let us remind ourselves that many, in fact, thought that Jesus was a false prophet. If we judge correctly, it is not fear of listening to a new call, but fear of not listening that should most concern us. The Bible itself has given us the standard by which to judge if a man is a prophet: by his fruits, what he brings forth, and by the truth of his words.[27] We should not be afraid to apply the standard.

In addition, we have the testimony of prophecy to help guide us in making decisions. The Bahá'í Faith has much to say about the meaning of prophecy. Indeed,

---

Cleobius and his Cleobienes, Dositheus and his Dositheans [who claimed to be a prophet like Moses], Gorthaeus and his Gorathenes, and the Masbotheans. From these were derived the Menandrianists, Marcionits, Carpocratians, Valentians, Basilidians, and Saturnilians, every man introducing his own opinion in his own particular way. From these in turn came false Christs, false prophets, false apostles, who split the unity of the church by poisoning suggestions against God and His Christ." *Eusebius, The History of the Church from Christ to Constantine* (New York: Penguin Books, 1965) p. 182.

27. *Matthew 7:15-20.* See also *Deuteronomy 13:1-3; 18:20-22.*

perhaps the first thing that becomes obvious in studying the Bahá'í Faith is not that Bahá'ís think the Lord will soon come, but that He has already come. And not once, but three times. This, as we shall soon disclose, is also the message of the Bible. Let us proceed now with this testimony and with further interpretation of prophecy.

Chapter 2

THE THREE ADVENTS IN PROPHECY

Have We Been Asleep Three Times?

Jesus once gathered His favored disciples and told them to watch while He went to pray. When Jesus returned He found them sleeping. Three times the Lord commanded them to watch and pray. Three painful times He returned to find them sleeping.[1] The verses read:

> And they came to a place which was named Gethsemane: and he saith to his disciples, Sit ye here, while I shall pray. And he taketh with him Peter and James and John, and began to be sore amazed, and to be very heavy; And saith unto them, My soul is exceedingly sorrowful unto death; tarry ye here, and watch. And he went forward a little, and fell on the ground, and prayed that, if it were possible, the hour might pass from him.

1. See *Matthew 26:40-46* and *Luke 22:45-46.*

THE SLEEPING DISCIPLES
in the Garden of Gethsemane. (*Matthew 14:32-41*)

> And he said, Abba, Father, all things are possible unto thee; take away this cup from me: nevertheless not what I will, but what thou will. *And he cometh, and findeth them sleeping*, and saith unto Peter, Simon, sleepest thou? couldst not thou watch one hour? Watch ye and pray, lest ye enter into temptation. The spirit truly is ready, but the flesh is weak. And again he went away, and prayed, and spake the same words. *And when he returned, he found them asleep again*, (for their eyes were heavy) neither wist they what to answer him. *And he cometh the third time, and saith unto them, Sleep on now*, and take your rest: it is enough the hour is come; behold the Son of man is betrayed into the hands of sinners. *Mark 14:32-41* (Emphasis mine.)

Is this simply a curious sad story about how hard it is for even good disciples to obey the Lord? Or is it a prophecy that relates to a shortcoming in the entire Christian community at the advent of the Lord? Consider the wording in the following verses that clearly refers to the coming of the Lord:

> Blessed are those servants whom the Lord, when he cometh, shall find them watching; verily I say unto you, that he shall gird himself, and make them sit down to eat, and will

> come forth and serve them. And if he shall come in the *second watch*, or come in the *third watch*, and find them so, blessed are those servants. *Luke 12:37-38* (Emphasis mine.)

Is it possible that this verse, like the one before, is trying to tell us more than that the Lord will come at night and it will be hard to stay awake? Could it be that, with all its marvelous detail, this is a prophecy that the Lord will come unto us in *each* of the three watches of the night. If this is so, then the prophecy indicates that some will find Him in each of these watches. For these, there will be blessings, and the Lord will share the food of His words with them and serve them. These believers are jewels which the Lord, like a thief in the night, will steal out of the house of humanity. The prophecy is clear, however, that most will not be awake during the watches of the night. For those who sleep, the prophecy indicates the harsh reality that they will be passed over.

Consider also that, in the prophecy, the Lord's advent (during one of the watches of the night) does not bring instant day. Rather, the darkness continues except for those few who find their day with the Lord's arrival. The rest of us are still in the night. Prophecy tells us that the Lord's first and second advent, in the watches of the night, will not bring instant daylight to all humanity. It is only with His final arrival at the break of day that light will dawn on us all, and then the mystery of what happened while we were sleeping will be revealed.

Jonah and the Three Days

When asked for a sign of proof of Who He was, Jesus answered with the Old Testament story of Jonah:

> Then certain of the scribes and of the Pharisees answered saying, Master, we would see a sign from thee. But He answered and said unto them, An evil and adulterous generation seeketh after a sign, and there shall no sign be given to it, but the sign of the prophet Jonah; For as Jonah was *three days and three nights* in the belly of the great fish, so shall the Son of man be three days and three nights in the heart of the earth. *Matthew 12:38-40* (Emphasis mine.)

Jonah was a reluctant prophet. In trying to escape his divine summons, he boarded a boat headed away from the land to which he was commanded to preach.[2] Yet God's will was greater. Jonah was tossed from the boat and swallowed by a great fish. For three days and three nights Jonah resided in that fish before being led to the destination God had determined for Him. Christ's reply to the one who challenged Him was sad and prophetic. The Messiah stood before him, and yet, he was being told, those who disbelieved would not receive the Mes-

2. *Jonah 1:1 ff, 2 Kings 14:25ff.*

JONAH RELEASED
after three days and three nights in the belly of a great fish. (See *Matthew 12:38-40*)

siah for three days and three nights. To what do these three days and nights refer?

They cannot refer to the time between Christ's crucifixion and resurrection, because the time interval is wrong. Jesus was crucified and died on a Friday evening and He rose (according to scripture) on Sunday morning. Even counting the days inclusively, this is only three days and two nights.

Few Christians fail to see how Jesus, the light of the world, brought daylight to mankind.[3] However, Christ's own testimony indicated that the time after His ministry would be like a night. Consider this verse:

> I must work the works of him that sent me, while it is day; the night cometh, when no man can work. As long as I am in the world, I am the light of the world. *John 9:4-5*

Similar passages are found elsewhere in John.[4] The Bahá'í writings also indicate that we can speak of the ministry of a Chosen One of God as a day and the time between the ministries of the Chosen Ones as a night.[5]

3. *John 8:12; 9:5.*

4. "Yet a little while is the light with you. Walk while ye have the light, lest darkness come upon you; for he that walketh in darkness knoweth not where he goeth." *John 12:35*

5. "By 'night' is meant the period between two divine Revelations when the Sun of Truth is not manifest among men." The Báb, *Selections from the Writings of the Báb* (Haifa: Bahá'í World Center, 1976) p. 129.

Thus we see that the ministry of Jesus may be counted as the first day, and the time after His ministry as the first night. But what about the second and third days and nights? Was Jesus trying to tell us that three appearances of the Sun would occur before humankind would find its Promised One? If Jesus was the bringer of the first day, who was the bringer of the second day and of the third? And where is the Promised One, that is, the bringer of the fourth day—not followed by night?

Three Sets of Messengers Before the Coming of the King

Consider the parable of the wedding feast of the king's son.[6] The wedding feast is a symbol of consummation, a joy in the future that can come only when man sits at the table promised by God. It is thus a prophecy that takes us to the end times. The parable indicates clearly that there were three sets of servants sent out before the coming of the king:

> The kingdom of heaven is like a certain king who made a marriage for his son, *And sent forth his servants* to call them that were bidden to the wedding; and they would not come. *Again he sent forth other servants*, saying, tell them who are bid-

6. *Matthew 22:1-14*. See also *Luke 14:15-24*.

den, Behold, I have prepared my dinner; my oxen and my fattlings are killed, and all things are ready; come unto the marriage. But they made light of it, and went their ways, one to his farm another to his merchandise; And the remnant took his servants, and treated them shamefully and slew them.

But when the king heard of it, he was angry; and he sent forth his armies, and destroyed those murderers, and burned up their city. *Then saith he to his servants*, The wedding is ready, but they who were bidden were not worthy.

Go therefore, into the highways, and as many as ye shall find, bid to the marriage. So that those servants went out into the highways, and gathered together all, as many as they found, both good and bad; and the wedding was furnished with guests. *And when the king came* in to see the guests, he saw there a man who had not on a wedding garment. And he saith unto him, Friend, how camest thou in here not having a wedding garment? And he was speechless. Then said the king to the servants, Bind him hand and foot, and take him away, and cast him into outer darkness; there shall be weeping and wailing and gnashing of teeth. . . *Matthew 22:2-13* (Emphasis mine.)

Note that in these verses servants were sent forth three times to call those bidden to the wedding feast before the king finally came. Jesus and His disciples called people to the kingdom of God and to the wedding feast prepared by God, the king. But those bidden would not come. This was the first call. What other calls to the wedding feast will be made before the King comes? Have these calls occurred?

Two Rains, Then the Harvest

Consider next the testimony in the Letter of James. James knew that Jesus had planted the seeds of hope among His followers for the day of restitution. But he announced the appearance of *two* divine waterings that would occur before the fruit of the promised day could be reaped:

> Be patient therefore, brethren, unto the coming of the Lord. Behold, the husbandman waiteth for the precious fruit of the earth, and hath long patience for it, until he receive the *early* and *latter* rain. Be ye also patient; stablish your hearts: for the coming of the Lord draweth nigh. *James 5:6-7* (Emphasis mine.)

If the harvest refers to the end times, what two divine waterings occurred after Jesus planted the seeds?

Three Measures Till the Whole is Leavened

Suppose that God had in mind to leaven the whole of humankind, which is like meal. Jesus certainly provided leaven to Christians, who are as one measure of the meal of humankind. But consider the prophecy of Christ in the next verses, in which we are told that leaven will be set to work on two other measures of meal:

> And again He said, "To what shall I liken the Kingdom of God? It is like leaven which a woman took and hid in three measures of meal, till the whole was leavened." *Luke 13:20-21*

If the leaven of the Holy Spirit is eternal and unchanging, these verses promise us that two other peoples, who are measures of meal, would receive the Holy Spirit after the time of Christ and before the whole of humankind is leavened. Who are these two other peoples through which the leaven of the Holy Spirit has worked? If we recognize them, are we near the time when the whole can be leavened?

In Three Days the Temple Shall Be Rebuilt

Now consider the verses which usually have been

applied to the time between the death and the resurrection of Christ:[7]

> Then answered the Jews, and said unto them, What sign showest thou unto us, seeing that thou doest these things? Jesus answered, and said unto them, Destroy this temple, and in three days I will raise it up. *John 3:18-19*

John, the evangelist, tells us that the Temple referred to the body of Jesus.[8] But what if the days in the prophecy were not literal days, but ages: the time between the coming of one Chosen One and the next. After all, as scripture reminds us, a day of God is not like a day of man.[9] Then the prophecy of the Temple would be similar to the prophecy of Jonah; to the prophecy of returning during the three watches of the night; to the three calls before the coming of the king to the wedding feast; to the three measures of meal; and to the three events before the harvest. Thus, the body of Jesus would return three times before the advent of the final day. This is, in fact, the claim of the Bahá'ís with respect to the prophecy of the Temple being rebuilt in three days.[10]

7. See also *Mark 14:58, 15:29*; *Matthew 26:62*, and *27:40.*

8. *John 2:22.*

9. "But beloved, be not ignorant of this one thing, that one day is with the Lord as a thousand years, and a thousand years as one day." *2 Peter 3:8*

10. Referring to His Revelation, Bahá'u'lláh writes, "Verily the

Christians and the Cock Crow

Finally, consider what may be much more than a simple story about Peter's behavior. Peter once denied Jesus three times. The verses read:

> Jesus said unto him, Verily I say unto thee that this night, before the cock crows, thou shalt deny me thrice. *Matthew 26:34*

Cocks crow at the break of day. If we understand that the break of day when the cock crows is another way of expressing the advent of the promised day of the Lord's advent, and if we recognize that Jesus was speaking to Peter as the representative of His church, then it becomes clear that this is a prophecy that Christians will deny their Lord three times before they recognize the dawn of the promised day. If it is true that the Lord has come three times since the day of Jesus and we have denied Him, then we have followed in the footsteps of Peter. Peter, however, after his denial in the night, arose to become the foundation for the new church. This may be our challenge as well.

Temple hath been built with the hands of the will of your Lord . . . This is the Temple promised you in the Tablets." Shoghi Effendi, *The Promised Day Is Come* (Wilmette, Il.: Bahá'í Publishing Trust, 1980) p. 47.

Threes in the Book of Revelation

Let us also consider the significance of "threes" in the Book of Revelation. Recall that Revelation is organized in sets of seven. There are seven churches, seven lamps, seven spirits, seven stars, seven candlesticks, and several other sets of seven as well. In accordance with standard biblical scholarship, I understand the number seven to be a symbol of totality or completeness, in the early sets of seven.[11] For example, Revelation begins with a long set of warnings to the seven churches about what would happen if they were not faithful to God. Thus, the warnings given to the seven churches, which happen to be in modern-day Turkey, apply to *all* churches.[12] Similarly, the seven spirits before God refer to all spirits before God. Many of the other sevens refer to completeness as well.

However, as Revelation progresses, it becomes clear that there are important divisions in some of the last sets of seven. For example, when the One on the throne

11. "Seven, the preeminently sacred number with the Hebrews and found also among other peoples, the one used typically in the scriptures in every conceivable relation and numberless instances, where fullness, completeness, certainty is thought of, is the favorite number with our author [of Revelation] and forms one of the dominant influences in his manner." Isbon T. Beckwith, *The Apocalypse of John* (Grand Rapids, MI: Baker Book House, 1979) p. 253.

12. There may be a significance to the location of the churches in this region as will become apparent when we discuss the identity and work of the first Advent after Jesus.

SETS OF SEVEN
in the Book of Revelation

SET OF 7 SEALS (Rev. 6)	INTERLUDE BETWEEN THE 6TH AND 7TH SEAL (Rev. 7)	SET OF 7 TRUMPET BLASTS (Rev. 8-11)
4 seals release the four horsemen of the apocalypse	4 angels hold back the winds of God's wrath	4 trumpet blasts cause destruction to nature
The 5th seal reveals that more servants will be killed	The 5th angel appears from the East with the seal of the Living God	5th trumpet blast
The 6th seal causes an earthquake and the light of the sun, moon, and stars to fail	A great multitude, washed in the blood of the Lamb, passes through a tribulation	6th trumpet blast
	7th seal opened	7th trumpet blast

of God holds out a scroll with seven seals, and the Lamb, whom I take to be Jesus, opens them one at a time, the breaking of the seals does not just represent totality. The seals are grouped into a set of four and a set of three. Similarly, in the interlude between the opening of the sixth and seventh seal, and in the sounding of the seven trumpets, other sets of seven are broken as shown in the table on page 39.[13]

In each case, the first four in each set of events are grouped together. Thus, we speak about the *four* horsemen of the apocalypse, the *four* angels that hold the *four* winds of God's wrath at the *four* corners of the earth (Revelation 7), and the first *four* trumpet blasts of Revelation 8, which are similar in that they harm only the natural world: the trees, grass, sea, rivers, and heavens. The remaining part of these sets are each distinct. The opening of the fifth, sixth, and seventh seal; the interlude; and the last three trumpet blasts, refer again to three Revelations which have occurred since the days of Jesus.[14] We will examine these Revelations, and their biblical references, one by one.[15]

13. It is not clear if the final set of seven (the seven bowls of wrath) is divided. Indeed, there is reason to believe that these bowls of wrath are not divided because the wrath appears to fall as a consequence of the appearance of the last (seventh) trumpet blast.

14. The Bahá'ís have no commentary available in English on the seven seals at this time. However, not all of the writings of Bahá'u'lláh or 'Abdu'l-Bahá have been translated, so authoritative commentary may be forthcoming. I have placed some of my own thoughts on the meaning of the seven seals in Appendix 1. Commentary on the fifth, sixth, and seventh trumpet blasts appears in text.

15. Finally, I understand that there are seven major holy days in the Jewish calendar. The fourth of these can be related to the ministry of Christ. The last three may be related to the ministries which followed.

Chapter 3

THE FIRST ADVENT AFTER JESUS

I have said that Jesus prophesied the coming of three prophets of God after Him. Who is the first prophet? It is the Book of Revelation that provides us with the most detail on this subject. We will pick up the story with the sounding of the trumpet blasts.[1]

Trumpet blasts were used by Moses to call the Jews to assemble, to alert them of troublous times, and to announce religious rites.[2] The prophet Joel commanded that the trumpet be blown as a sign of God's judgment against his people at the arrival of the day of the Lord.[3] Revelation tells us the last three of the seven trumpet blasts were special. The verses read:

> And I beheld, and heard an angel flying through the midst of heaven, saying with a loud voice, Woe, woe, woe, to the inhabiters

1. The story may begin as early as the fifth seal. I have placed some notes of my thoughts on this in Appendix 1. However, as Bahá'ís have authoritative commentary on the trumpet blasts of Revelation, I am picking up the subject at this point.

2. *Numbers 10:1-10.*

3. *Joel 2:1.*

> of the earth by reason of the other voices of the trumpet of the three angels, *which are yet to sound! Revelation 8:13* (Emphasis mine.)

Each of these last trumpet blasts is an arrival of the day of the Lord. Each was a woe to humankind much as the voice of Jesus was a woe to those who disbelieved in Him and the judgment to come.[4]

The Fifth Trumpet Blast

The fifth trumpet blast, according to Bahá'í teaching, represents the first divine Revelation after the time of Jesus. The verses which introduce this Revelation read:

> And the fifth angel sounded, and I saw a star fall from heaven unto the earth and to him was given the key to the bottomless pit. And he opened the bottomless pit, and there arose a smoke out of the pit, like the smoke of a great furnace; and the sun and air were darkened by reason of the smoke of the pit. And there came out of the smoke locusts upon the earth, and unto them was given power, as the scorpions of the earth have power. And it was commanded them that they should not hurt the grass of the earth, neither any green thing,

4. See *Matthew 11:21*; *18:7*; and *23:13-29.*

> neither any tree, only those men who have not the seal of God in their foreheads. *Revelation 9:1-4*

Here is a strange vision. A being from heaven is sent to earth to open the gate over the pit of hell. Smoke rises from the pit and darkens the sky. Terrible locusts come from the smoke, yet these locusts do the work of God: They attack only those who do not have the seal of God. The king of the locust, we are later told, is called "the Destroyer," but what is destroyed are those who are not sealed. Thus the appellation symbolizes His work as an agent of God's justice.

Christian interpreters have attached every possible identity to the star that falls from the sky. The star has been called Satan, because he is seen to "fall from heaven" and because he is a destroyer.[5] He has been called a messenger of God because he does God's work.[6] Although it is possible to take either interpreta-

5. For example, Hal Lindsay, *There's a New World Coming*, (New York: Bantam Books, 1984) pp. 121-122.

6. "The one symbolized by the star has been variously identified. Some, interpreting the phrase 'from heaven fallen' in a theological sense, take the star to be a fallen angel. This is strengthened by reference to the nefarious nature of his activity (unlocking the shaft of the abyss and releasing its demonic hordes). Perhaps he is one of the stars of heaven swept down to earth by the tail of the great red dragon (12:4). It is more likely, however, that the star-angel is simply one of the many divine agents who throughout the book of Revelation are pictured as carrying out the will of God. Charles shows that when applied to stars symbolizing angels, 'to fall' means no more than 'to descend' (I, pp.238-

tion from a Bahá'í perspective, it is more likely the star represents a Messenger of God.[7] This is because Bahá'ís believe that the fifth angel's trumpet blast refers to the Revelation of Muḥammad,[8] the Prophet of God.

Why do we in the West find it so difficult to be fair in our judgments about Muḥammad and His religion? The reasons are not hard to find. Because we made Jesus the sole occupant on the throne of God, there is no room for anyone else. Yet in Revelation, Jesus is but a lamb before the throne of God and there are other agents of God's will in this drama who must be identified. Revelation speaks clearly of prophet/witnesses

---

239). Furthermore, his role is not essentially different from that of the fifth trumpet-angel at whose call the action begins. He is probably the same angel who in 20:1 comes down out of heaven with the key of the abyss." R.H. Mounce, *The New International Commentary on the Book of Revelation* (Wm B. Eerdmans Publishing Co., 1977) pp. 192-193. "The star of our passage is an agent sent from heaven in the service of God; cf. Rev 20:1. The identification with him with Satan, based on a comparison of Lk. 10:18 with Rev 12:9 (so, Alford, *al*) is certainly wrong; Satan nowhere appears in the book as an agent employed by God to carry out a divine ordering, such as sending this plague upon the world." Beckwith, *The Apocalypse of John*, pp. 560-561.

7. Bahá'ís may interpret the star as being a worker of evil by identifying the Umayyad leader of society that opposed Muḥammad as the falling star. Muḥammad would then be the sun whose light was darkened by the smoke arising from the pit which the Umayyad leader opened.

8. "The first woe is the appearance of the Prophet Muḥammad, the son of 'Abdu'lláh—peace be upon Him!" ('Abdu'l-Bahá, *Some Answered Questions*, (Wilmette, Il.: Bahá'í Publishing Trust, 1984) p. 56.

who will appear before the coming of the Promised One. Is it not possible that Muḥammad is one of these prophets? To the almost one billion Muslims on the planet, it is simply a statement of fact that after the ministry of Jesus, God continued His redemptive work through another Prophet: Muḥammad.

The Mission of Muḥammad

While Islam is a complex religion, attending to the spiritual as well as the social needs of man, one of its prime aims was to rid the world of polytheism.[9] The Islamic profession of faith says, "There is no God but God, and Muḥammad is His Messenger."[10] Prior to Muḥammad's ministry, the central building of Mecca was filled with idols. Mecca was a trading city, and the city fathers perceived it as important to offer a home to the god of every village, city, and country that traded in Mecca. Muḥammad was commanded to call the Arabs and all peoples to the one true God and to cast out the idols.

Both Arabs and Jews are Semites, and both are descendants of Abraham, the father of nations. Today, the central building of Mecca which once was filled with idols, is the kaaba (*ka'bah*) of Islam, the place toward

9. Another was to build larger units of theocracy: nations under God. See Shoghi Effendi, *Promised Day Is Come*, p. 120.

10. Qur'an 2:163 and 48:29.

which Muslims turn in prayer. It contains a single, large black stone, placed there in remembrance of Abraham, the forefather of the Arabs.[11]

Abram (later Abraham) had three wives. When the first, Sarai (later Sarah), bore Him no children, Sarai gave her Egyptian slave Hagar to Abraham as a wife to beget His children. Hagar beget Ishmael, and of course Sarai became jealous and mistreated Hagar. The Lord saw this injustice and vowed that He would use the descendants of Ishmael as an agent for reproving the descendants of Sarah.[12] Sarah later was made fertile and produced Abraham's son Isaac. The Jews are descended from Isaac; the Arabs trace their descent from Ishmael. A descendent of Abraham's third wife, Katurah, is the founder of the Bahá'í Faith.[13]

Why Not a Christian Messenger

The work of Sarah's descendants might have completed God's redemptive work with humanity had it not been

11. The stone is said to have been brought to Abraham by Gabriel from paradise.

12. "And the angel of the Lord said unto her [Hagar], I will multiply thy seed exceedingly, that it shall not be numbered for multitude. And the angel of the Lord said unto her, Behold thou art with child, and shalt bear a son, and shalt call his name Ishmael; because the Lord hath heard thy affliction. And he will be a wild man, and his hand will be against every man, and every man's hand against him; and he shall dwell in the presence of all his brethren". *Genesis 16:10-12*

13. See Shoghi Effendi, *God Passes By*, p. 94.

that 600 years after the appearance of Jesus, God called upon the descendants of Ishmael to do His bidding. Is this strange? Why didn't God call the Christians next? Because Jesus was sent specifically to the lost sheep of Israel, and to them alone.[14] When they rejected the message and the Messenger, the divine favor returned to the seed of Abraham, where, according to the Old Testament, it would always lie.[15] Gentile Christians are children of God by adoption, but there were others, related by blood, who had been promised a renewed relationship.[16]

The book of Genesis (16:12) characterized Ishmael as a wild man. And so did God find the descendants of Ishmael at the time of Muḥammad. They were a hardy, near-savage people who buried infant daughters alive and whom history records as having had 1,700 battles prior to the time of Muḥammad.[17] Yet, God had promised to make them a great nation.[18] The biblical

14. "But he [Jesus] answered [the Canaanite woman] and said, 'I am not sent but unto the lost sheep of the house of Israel.' " *Matthew 15:24*

15. "And I will establish my covenant between me [God] and thee [Abraham] and thy seed after thee in their generations for an everlasting covenant, to be a God unto thee, and to thy seed after thee." *Genesis 17:7*

16. The fact that Christians are "adopted" by God is spoken of by Paul. For example, we read, "For ye [the Roman Christians] have not received the spirit of bondage again to fear; but ye have received the Spirit of adoption, whereby we cry, Abba, Father." *Romans 8:15*. See also *Galatians 4:4*.

17. Edward Gibbon, *The Decline and Fall of the Roman Empire* (New York: The Modern Library, n.d.) Vol. 3, p. 67.

18. "And as for Ishmael, I [God] have heard thee [Abraham]:

prophecy of the fifth trumpet blast foretold the role that this nation would play.

Opposition and Battle

We think first of a prophet bringing us the keys of heaven. But a prophet may also bring us the keys of hell. The Book of Revelation clarifies this point when it states (Revelation 1:18), "I [one like the Son of Man] am he that liveth, and was dead; and behold, I am alive for evermore, Amen, *and have the keys of hades and of death.*" When the fifth angel of Revelation sounded his trumpet, the star that came to earth (Muḥammad) opened first the pit of hell. He did not descend into hell, nor was he from hell. Rather he allowed those that were in hell to ascend to earth and be judged. It is in interaction with God's Chosen One that our true state is most clearly revealed. Muḥammad judged these who rose against him.

When the pit was opened, we are told, smoke, like the smoke of a great furnace, arose and darkened the sun and air. This is the smoke of opposition and its most significant characteristic is that it obscures our view. We in the West are still looking through a glass

---

behold, I have blessed him, and will make him fruitful, and will multiply him exceedingly; twelve princes shall he beget, and I will make him a great nation." *Genesis 17:21*. See also *Genesis 21:18*. More will be said about the twelve princes presently.

darkly when we contemplate Islam. Muḥammad was met by a fire-storm of opposition determined to obscure His light. This opposition shaped the character of Islam. It necessitated that the first teachers of Islam would be soldiers, not disciples. And this gives us a key to another symbol used in Revelation: the locusts.

The locusts that appear out of the smoke are the soldiers of Islam. They do not come up from the pit; rather they appear because of the opposition of those who are from the pit. Had the early Muslims not defended themselves, there would be no Islam today. The idol worshipers would not have left a single one alive. The Old Testament prophet Joel used locusts as a symbol for the agents of God's justice.[19] In Revelation we see this same symbol similarly employed. We are told, "the shapes of the locusts were like horses prepared unto battle; and on their heads were, as it were, crowns like gold, and their faces were like the faces of men."[20] These are the soldiers of Islam going forth on their mission: to remove the bane of polytheism from the earth, to reprove those who had not God's "seal," that is, those who were not Christians or Jews. Good people of the Book, Jews and Christians who did no wrong, the Qur'an makes plain, were to be protected from God's wrath against polytheist. The verses read:

19. See Joel 1-2. Locusts also are used in *Exodus 10:12* ff as a means of bringing God's punishment to Egypt.

20. *Revelation 9:7.*

> Do not dispute with the People of the Book save in the fairer manner, except for those that do wrong; and say, "We believe in what has been sent down to us, and what has been sent down to you; our God and your God is One, and to Him we have surrendered."
> *Qur'an 29:46*

Curiously, we learn from Revelation (9:4) that the locust warriors were told "that they should not hurt the grass of the earth, neither any green thing, neither any tree . . ." Abú-Bakr, the first caliph, and sometime commander of the Islamic armies, echoed the precise instructions of the Bible as he spoke to his soldiers prior to an expedition to Syria. He said:

> You are always in the presence of God, on the verge of death, in the assurance of judgment, and the hope of paradise. Avoid injustice and oppression; consult with your brethren, and study to preserve the love and confidence of your troops. When you fight the battles of the Lord, acquit yourself like men, without turning your backs; but let not your victory be stained with the blood of women and children. Destroy no palm-trees, nor burn any fields of corn. Cut down no fruit-trees, nor do any mischief to cattle, only such as you kill to eat. When you make any covenant or article, stand to it, and be as good as your word. As you go on, you will find some religious persons who live retired in monasteries, and

propose to themselves to serve God in that way: let them alone, and neither kill them nor destroy their monasteries: and you will find another sort of people, that belong to the synagogue of Satan, who have shaven crowns; be sure you cleave their skulls, and give them no quarter till they either turn Mohammadans or pay tribute.[21]

The Sword of Islam

The enemies of Islam have painted a picture of a faith spread by the sword and somehow inferior to Christianity, the religion of love. These people conveniently forget that for centuries Christians had no hesitation about spreading their religion by force. In addition, it is simply untrue that Islam was spread primarily by force. The Qur'an itself forbids forced religion:

> No compulsion is there in religion. Rectitude had become clear from error. So whoever disbelieves in idols and believes in God, has laid hold of the most firm handle, unbreaking; God is All-hearing, All-knowing. *Qur'an 2:257*

This does not mean, however, that Muslims tolerated idol worshipers or unfaithful Christians and Jews.

21. Gibbon, *The Decline and Fall of the Roman Empire*, Vol. 3, p. 145.

They did not. But the sword with which the unrepentant were punished is the same sword that was promised them in the Bible. Note that the Book of Revelation repeatedly warned the seven churches that if they fell back into idolatry, violent retribution awaited them. The Muslim armies that later swept into the lands of the seven churches exercised this selective judgment exactly as the Bible had foretold.[22] Many of those who had fallen from faith were, in the words of the gospel, "cut asunder."[23] The sword of Islam was very real, but was not different from the sword of both the Old and the New Testaments. In fact, it was the one foretold by them. However, we in the West, with our myopic vision, still have failed to understand that Islam is a part of Christian prophecy. We do not recognize Islam as part of God's plan because it goes by a different name. But that, too, had been foretold in prophecy.[24]

22. Recall that the seven churches of the Book of Revelation were in lands which were later purified by Islam.

23. "The lord of that servant [who eats and drinks with the drunkards] shall come in a day when he looketh not for him, and in an hour that he is not aware of, and shall cut him asunder, and appoint him his portion with the hypocrites; and there shall be weeping and gnashing of teeth." *Matthew 24:50-51*

24. For example, Revelation 2:17 says, "He that hath an ear let him hear what the Spirit saith unto the churches: To him that overcometh will I give to eat of the hidden manna, and will give him a white stone, and in the stone a new name written, which no man knoweth except he that receiveth it."

The 150 Years of Islamic Expansion

The verses in the Book of Revelation indicate that the locusts would have power for five months.[25] This is the literal average life-span of a locust, and may indicate simply that the Islamic armies would have power for a time that was natural to them. However, some Bahá'ís have noted that the five months (150 days) could be reckoned 150 years by the day-for-a-year formula commonly used by both biblical scholars.[26] In this case, the meaning would be that Islamic armies would advance for about 150 years. This corresponds well with the history of the expansion of Islam. When the smoke of battle finally cleared a Muslim civilization arose which would be the light of the world for over 500 years.

The prophecy of the locust was fulfilled almost 1,300 years ago. Even today, Islamic warriors still feel that they are on guard against any irreligious excess. We will discuss this again in the chapters to come.

25. *Revelation 9:5.*

26. See Ruth Moffett, *New Keys to the Book of Revelation*, (New Delhi: Bahá'í Publishing Trust, 1977) chapter nine. She counts the years as referring to the rule of the Umayyads.

A MIGHTY ANGEL
A literal interpretation by the artist. (*Revelation 10:1-4*)

Chapter 4

A VISION BEYOND ISLAM

As we shall see, the Book of Revelation has more to say about Islam. After describing the locust warriors, however, it skips ahead briefly to give us a vision of our ultimate goal: the Revelations beyond Islam. The Revelation of Muḥammad was the fifth trumpet blast and the first woe for the unbelievers after the Revelation of Jesus. The book now reminds us, "there are two woes more hereafter."[1] Chapters 9 and 10 of the Book of Revelation thus provide a quick sketch of what is to come in these next two Revelations, which are intertwined. The passage begins with the sixth trumpet blast:

> And the sixth angel sounded, and I heard a voice from the four horns of the golden altar which is before God, Saying to the sixth angel who had the trumpet, Loose the four angels who are bound in the great river, Euphrates. And the four angels were loosed, who were prepared for an hour, and a day, and a month, and a year, to slay the third part of

1. *Revelation 9:12.*

> men. And the number of the army of the horsemen were two hundred thousand thousand; and I heard the number of them. And thus I saw the horse in the vision, and them that sat on them, having breastplates of fire, and of jacinth, and brimstone; and the heads of the horses were like the heads of lions, and out of their mouths issued fire and smoke and brimstone. By these three was the third part of men killed, by fire, and by the smoke, and by the brimstone, which issued out of their mouths. For their power is in their mouth, and in their tails; for their tails were like serpents, and had heads, and with them they do hurt. And the rest of the men who were not killed by these plagues yet repented not of the works of their hands, that they should not worship demons, and idols of gold, and silver, and bronze, and stone, and wood, which neither can see, nor hear, nor walk. Neither repented they of their murders, nor of their sorceries, nor of their fornication, nor of their thefts. *Revelation 9:13-21*

A Judgment Against Us

There are significant differences between this judgment and the one that occurred at the sounding of the fifth trumpet which announced the appearance of Islam. The wrath unleashed during the dispensation of Islam was focused against a particular people, those idol worshipers who were not Jews and Christians. This time the forces of destruction fall upon all. There is no restraining general commanding, "do not hurt the people of the Book or any green thing."

In this judgment, it is the materialism of humankind that is being condemned. It is the work of they who "repented not of the works of their hands, that they should not worship demons and idols of gold, and silver, and bronze, and stone, and wood, which neither can see, nor hear, nor walk." It is also our misdeeds: "Neither repented they of their murders, nor of their sorceries, nor of their fornication, nor of their thefts." Of these sins, all humankind is guilty. It is no wonder then that the scope of the retribution in these verses is vast.

In the Midst of Judgment

It seems curious that so much is made of the date of the beginning of these tragedies. There is a preciseness involved, a clock set to strike at a given moment, an hour, a day, a month, a year. Has the hour come and the penalties been unleashed? Have we not seen in our modern age wars and horrors of apocalyptic dimensions?

What the Bahá'ís say here is not that these horrors have passed, nor that they are a prelude to a second coming, but that the world is in the *midst* of judgment, a judgment that may reach a dreadful climax! The judgment, which began in 1844 with the sounding of the sixth trumpet blast, is the result of our failure to respond to the Prophets that appeared after Muḥammad. As a consequence, the winds of God's wrath—according to Revelation, previously held in check—have now been unleashed and we are being punished for our general waywardness. The Guardian of the Bahá'í Faith writes:

> A tempest, unprecedented in its violence, unpredictable in its course, catastrophic in its immediate effects, unimaginably glorious in its ultimate consequences, is at present sweeping the face of the earth . . . Bewildered, agonized and helpless, it watches *this great and mighty wind of God* invading the remotest and fairest regions of the earth, rocking its foundations, deranging its equilibrium, sundering its nations, disrupting the homes of its peoples, wasting its cities, driving into exiles its kings, pulling down its bulwarks, uprooting its institutions, dimming its light, and harrowing up the souls of its inhabitants.[2]

The mechanism of this punishment are, as Revelation indicates, often the tools of our own design. They include the wars which rage around us as we fail to curb our desires and evil machinations and fail also to listen to the Word of God. These wars, which reached world-

2. Shoghi Effendi, *The Promised Day Is Come*, p. 3. (Emphasis mine.)

wide dimensions after 1844, will doubtless continue and may end in apocalyptic catastrophe. Bahá'u'lláh writes:

> We have fixed a time for you, O peoples. If ye fail, at the appointed hour, to turn towards God, He, verily, will lay violent hold on you, and will cause grievous afflictions to assail you from every direction.[3]

The Last Angel

The author of the Book of Revelation does not elaborate in Chapters 9 and 10 on the details of this Revelation after Muḥammad's. He merely pauses to forewarn us of the magnitude of the judgment which must follow the dispensation of Islam. And before returning to his consideration of Islam, he provides a glimpse of our hope: the arrival of the Promised One, a Prophet after Muḥammad, in the form of a mighty angel. The verses read:

> And I saw another mighty angel come down from heaven, clothed with a cloud; and a rainbow was upon his head, and his face was as though it were the sun, and his feet like pillars of fire. And he had in his hand a little scroll open; and he set his right foot upon the

3. *Gleanings from the Writings of Bahá'u'lláh*, p. 214.

> sea, and his left foot on the earth. And cried with a loud voice, as when a lion roareth; and when he had cried, seven thunders uttered their voices. And when the seven thunders had uttered their voices, I was about to write; and I heard a voice from heaven saying unto me, Seal up those things which the seven thunders uttered, and write them not. *Revelation 10:1-4*

This is a curious Angel. One commentator writes, "One cannot help but notice the similarities between John's description of the angel and that of Yahweh in Ezekiel 1:26-28."[4] The Angel also has characteristics ascribed to God Himself. He is dressed in a cloud;[5] there is a rainbow upon His head;[6] His face is as the sun;[7] His feet are as pillars of fire;[8] He roars with the voice of a lion;[9] thunder accompanies His voice;[10] and, like God, He has authority over both the sea and the earth. I will discuss the identity and work of this Angel later. But note that He appears during the ministry of the sixth angel—that is, before the seventh angel sounds His

4. Mounce, *The New International Commentary on the New Testament: The Book of Revelation* p. 206.
5. See *Psalms 104:3*
6. *Revelation 4:3.*
7. *Revelation 1:16.*
8. *Exodus 13:21.*
9. *Hosea 11:10; Amos 3:8.*
10. *Psalms 29:3-9.*

trumpet—and that He seems to represent, in a way never seen before, God Himself. We will see later that this mighty Angel is, in fact, the One who will sound the seventh trumpet blast.

A Story Too Important to Tell Once

The first fourteen verses of Revelation, Chapter 11, supply a vision which interrupts the sequence of trumpet blasts. Then, in verse fifteen, the seventh angel finally sounds. Thereafter follows a vision which seems to be another interruption in the natural sequence of events associated with the seventh angel's sounding. Much has been written about these two complex chapters. The reason for the seeming interruption of the last three trumpet blasts never has been understood. But the role of the two visions surrounding the seventh trumpet blast actually is quite simple. These visions retell the story of the fifth, sixth, and seventh trumpet blasts, each time adding more detail. The story is so important that it is retold three times. We turn now to examining Chapter 11, which returns us to Islam.

THE TWO WITNESSES
lying dead in the street for three days and a half. (*Revelation 11:1-14*)

Chapter 5

THE TWO WITNESSES OF THE FIRST ADVENT

In the Book of Revelation, after the sixth angel has blown his trumpet and before the seventh and last angel sounds, there is a vision of a temple, two prophet/witnesses, and a beast. The vision seems to be an interruption in the sequence of trumpet blasts, and the reason for this never has been clear. Accordingly, this chapter has been difficult for Christian interpreters. Henry Alford, Dean of Canterbury, once wrote: "No solution has ever been given to this portion of prophecy."[1] Another leading scholar writes: "This paragraph, 11:1-13, the second part of the interlude [between the sixth and seventh trumpet blasts] contains a vision to which it is confessedly difficult to assign a meaning and place appropriate in our book."[2] Others, too, note its difficulty.[3] The difficulties are both in interpreting symbols

1. "Apocalypse of John" in *The Greek Testament*, IV (Chicago: Moody, 1958) p. 658.

2. Beckwith, *The Apocalypse of John*, p. 584.

3. "Most commentators note that Chapter 11 is especially difficult to interpret." Mounce, *Commentary on the New Testament: The Book of Revelation*, p. 218.

and in identifying the characters. The beginning verses read:

> And there was given me a reed like a rod; and the angel stood, saying, Rise, and measure the temple of God, and the altar, and them that worship in it. But the court, which is outside the temple, leave out, and measure it not; for it is given unto the nations, and the holy city shall they tread under foot forty and two months. *Revelation 11:1-2*

John is commanded in the vision to measure the temple, the altar, and them that worship at it with a reed.[4] But what is the temple? Some Christian scholars, prone to literal interpretations, have argued that this verse refers to a physical temple which will be rebuilt just before the Second Coming at the site of the old temple in Jerusalem.[5] This reading fails because it attempts to combine a literal interpretation of a few words in a

4. Solomon's temple had two courts (1 Kings 6:36); Herod's had three, one for women, one for men, and one for priests. As the prophecy makes plain, the function of the inner court (no matter of how many divisions) was to separate it from the outer court. Josephus notes (*Bell*, v5:2) that there was a barrier between the inner and outer courts with an inscription threatening death to Gentiles who passed over it. The altar probably is the altar of burnt offering, the one before which the Israelites were supposed to gather.

5. See Hal Lindsay, *There's a New World Coming.*

verse with other words that make no sense when translated literally. For example, if the temple is a physical one, are the reed, the angel, the measurement, and the time frame also to be taken literally? Do angels command people to measure temples with reeds? What would be the meaning of this? Furthermore, rebuilding the temple on its original site would necessitate removing one of Islam's holiest shrines. It seems highly unlikely that the old temple will ever be rebuilt.

A symbolic interpretation is not only more likely, but richer in meaning. As Bahá'í writings suggest, the temple is a symbol for religion itself, with its two components: the inner court, or spiritual reality of a religion, and the outer court, the form of a religion.[6] The measurement is done by the Prophet of God, who is the

6. The symbolic meaning is explained in Bahá'í writings as follows: "The Law of God is divided into two parts. One is the fundamental basis which comprises all spiritual things—that is to say, it refers to spiritual virtues and divine qualities; this does not change nor alter: it is the Holy of Holies, which is the essence of the Law of Adam, Noah, Abraham, Moses, Christ, Muḥammad, the Báb and Bahá'u'lláh, and which lasts and is established in all the prophetic cycles . . . These divine qualities, these eternal commandments, will never be abolished; nay, they will last and remain forever and ever. These virtues of humanity will be renewed in each of the different cycles [of religion]; for at the end of every cycle the spiritual Law of God—that is to say, the human virtues—disappears, and only the form subsists." The outer court of religion is "the expression used for the form of religion." This second part of religion, the form, consists of observances such as "fasting, prayer, forms of worship, marriage, divorce, the abolition of slavery, legal processes, transactions, indemnities for

assayer of true religion. The reed is a symbol for the Prophet of God from Whom God's melody flows. The rod is the rod of His commandments. The prophecy is of a judgment. Those who are spiritually awake and live in the inner court of religion are counted by the assayer. Those who have only the form of the religion—the part dominated by laws, customs, rites, and rituals—are not counted. But which religion are we talking about?

The answer comes with the next verses, when the divine assayers are identified. Two prophet-witnesses are introduced:[7]

> And I will give power *unto my two witnesses*, and they shall prophesy a thousand two hundred and threescore days, clothed in sackcloth. *These are the two olive trees, and the two lamp stands standing before the God of the earth.* And if any man will hurt them, fire proceedeth out of their mouth, and devoureth their enemies; and if any man will hurt them, he must in this manner be killed. These have power to shut heaven, that it rain not in the days of their prophecy; and have power over

---

murder, violence, theft, and injuries—this part of the Law of God which refers to material things, is modified and altered in each prophetic cycle in accordance with the necessities of the times." 'Abdu'l-Bahá, *Some Answered Questions*, pp. 47-48.

7. The word "witness" is a pliable one in the New Testament. It is used of Jesus (*Revelation 1:5*) and of His disciple John (*Revelation 1:2*). It is also used of believers (e.g., *Acts 22:15*).

> waters to turn them to blood, and to smite the earth with all plagues, as often as they will.
> *Revelation 11:3-6* (Emphasis mine.)

The witnesses are characteristic of Old-Testament prophets. They have powers ascribed to Moses and Elijah, yet, as they are in the Book of Revelation, we know they appear after the ministry of Christ.[8] Their similarity to Moses and Elijah is significant because these are the prophets the Jews expect to return at the end of time. However, when they appear in the verses above, no mention is made of the end times. This will come later, when they reappear. Who are these two witnesses?

They are Muḥammad and 'Alí, his son-in-law and legitimate successor. They are dressed in sackcloth, the biblical symbol of mourning, because they mourn for humankind's unrepentance.[9] When they appear, as the prophecy foretold, people rose up against them and they received no help from either Jews or Christians. Jews and Christians have traditionally ignored or maligned Muḥammad and 'Alí and their work.

Even the words "witness" and "olive trees," which make up this part of prophecy, are used and defined in the Qur'an. Observe:

8. They have the powers of Moses as in *Exodus 7:17-21* and *Deuteronomy 18:15-18*, and the powers of Elijah as in *1 Kings 17:1* and *Malachi 4:5-6*.

9. *Matthew 11:212* and *Jeremiah 4:8*.

> Thus we [God] appoint you [the Muslim believers] a midmost nation that you might be witnesses to the people, and that the Messenger [Muḥammad] might be a *witness* to you. *Qur'an 2:143* (Emphasis mine.)

> God is the Light of the heavens and the earth; the likeness of His Light is as a niche wherein is a lamp [the lamp in a glass, the glass as it were a glittering star] kindled from a Blessed Tree, an *olive* that is neither of the East nor of the West whose oil wellnigh would shine, even if no fire touched it; Light upon Light (God guides to His Light whom He will). *Qur'an 24:35* (Emphasis mine.)

Thus Muḥammad and 'Alí are both witnesses and olive trees who produce the sacred oil which is neither of the East nor of the West.

We are now in a position to answer the question, "To what religion does the temple refer?" It refers to all of the semitic religions. As we have seen, Muḥammad and 'Alí evaluated both Jews and Christians, the People of the Book. But they also measured the faith of those who professed to be Muslims. As we shall see, opposition to Muḥammad and to 'Alí from within Islam is the subject of a major portion of biblical prophecy.

We in the West have had a hard time seeing Islam as

an extension of God's work foretold in the Bible. We object to the violence in Islam. We say it is too "Old-Testament" in character. Yet the Book of Revelation reminds us that the prophets of Islam are like those of the Old Testament and that the violence we see in Islam is directed and sanctioned by God.

The Significance of 'Alí

There is great significance in the fact that two witnesses, not one, are introduced in the verses above. Indeed, if we fail to understand the role of this second witness, much of the rest of prophecy and history is not interpretable.

'Alí was the first or second to believe in Muḥammad.[10] 'Alí was the son of Abú-Tálib, Muḥammad's uncle who had raised Muḥammad. During a severe famine Muḥammad persuaded His wife that they should adopt His cousin 'Alí, so as to ease the financial burden on His uncle. It is said that Muḥammad, His wife, and His cousin would often retreat into the desert to offer thanks to the Lord for His bounties to them.[11]

Muḥammad and 'Alí are not to be treated as equals.

10. Khadiját, Muḥammad's wife, is counted by some as the first.

11. Ameer 'Alí, *The Spirit of Islam: A History of the Evolution and Ideals of Islam*, (New Delhi: B.I. Publications, 1922) p. 20.

While they are both prophet-witnesses, Muḥammad was the Prophet of God. He was the chosen intermediary between God and man. His Light was independent of all others. 'Alí was a great man, a prophet with a lower-case "p." He can be seen as an intermediary between Muḥammad and the believers. His light was dependent upon the Light of Muḥammad. 'Alí was to Muḥammad what Joshua was to Moses, an accomplished general and His appointed successor.[12]

1260 Days of Islam

These two witnesses were to prophecy for forty-two months. The cycle of 1,260 days—expressed in its variant forms of forty-two months or three and a half years—is a recurrent biblical theme.[13] The meaning of the 1,260 days has remained obscure. From 167 to 164 B.C., the Greek king Antiochus IV (Epiphanes), occupied Jerusalem and desecrated its temple. Bible

12. Joshua's appointment by Moses to lead the people of Israel is found in Deuteronomy 31:7. 'Abdu'l-Bahá makes the comparison between Moses and Joshua and Muḥammad and 'Alí in *Some Answered Questions*, pp. 48-49.

13. Twelve hundred and sixty days is referenced in Revelation 11:3 and 12:6; forty-two months is found in Revelation 11:2 and 13:5; and three and a half years is found in Revelation 12:14, and Daniel 7:25 and 12:7. Three and a half years is translated as times, time and half a time in the King James Version, but the *New Schofield Reference Bible* of the King James Version mentions in the footnotes that "a time" is equivalent to "a year." The *New English Bible* translates a "time" as a "year."

scholars have speculated that the 1,260 day symbol for desolation may have been triggered by the approximately three and a half years of occupation by the Greek king.[14] However, the Book of Revelation speaks of events which are to occur *after* the ministry of Christ not before.

To what 1,260 days do these prophecies refer? The answer comes through a simple transformation and a simple application. The Bible itself gives us the clue to this transformation when it exchanges years for days. Thus, the Hebrews received forty years of penalty, one for each day they spent exploring Canaan.[15] The reckoning of days in prophecy to years in real time has been practiced widely by Bible scholars.[16] Thus, the

14. *The New English Bible* (footnotes to 1 Maccabbees 1:59 and 4:36-61) sets the date for the desecration of the temple at December 17, 167 B.C., and the date for rededicated December 164 B.C. Potok (*Wanderings*, New York,Alfred A. Knopf, 1978) sets the desecration date between April and December of 167 and the rededication date as October 16, 164. Considering these two estimates, the period of desolation was between three and three and a half years. Isbon T. Beckwith (*The Apocalypse of John*, 1919, pp. 252ff) notes the other major interpretation (put forth by Guntel) as being a reference to the approximately three and a half months of winter—a symbol of spiritual cold and desolation. He notes that the interpretation that it refers to a broken seven is considered improbable.

15. "After the number of the days in which ye searched the land, even forty days, each day for a year, shall ye bear your inequities, even forty years" (Numbers 14:34). 'Abdu'l-Bahá explains that the day in prophecy refers to a year. (*Some Answered Questions,* p. 40.)

16. The practice of interpreting a day as a year in real time is

1,260 days actually refers to 1,260 years. All we must do now is apply these years to the most obvious place: the beginning of the Muslim Era. Thus, the years begin with the dawn of the Muslim Era in 622 A.D., and end 1,260 lunar years later, at the Muslim year 1,260, which is Christian year 1844.[17] According to the Bahá'í Faith, the legitimate length of the Islamic Dispensation is 1,260 years. We will soon discuss what happened in the Muslim year 1260 A.H., the Christian year 1844 A.D.

---

very old and widespread among Bible scholars. One writer notes that the practice has been used by Augustine, Tichonius, Primasius, Andrea, the Venable Bede, Ambrosius, Ansbertus, Berengaud, and Bruno Astensis, besides the leading modern expositors. (Edward B. Elliot, *Horae Apocalypticae* Vol. 3, p. 234, notes 2-6; in Uriah Smith, *Daniel and the Revelation* [Washington, D.C.: Review and Herald Publishing Association, 1944] p. 204.) This practice has also been used by John Calvin, *Commentaries on the Book of the Prophet Daniel*, Vol 2, (Edinburgh: Calvin Translation Society, 1853) p. 196ff.

17. Here we will use the Islamic lunar calendar of reckoning years, not solar years used earlier. This is because the verses themselves call for the Islamic calendar: the prophecy is about Islam and, as will be seen, the exact starting place of the Islamic calendar will soon be revealed in the Bible. When we need Gregorian calendar dates for this part of prophecy, we will simply translate the Muslim year to the Gregorian year.

Chapter 6

THE BEAST OF THE FIRST ADVENT

How would humankind receive Muḥammad and 'Alí, the two prophets sent after the time of Jesus, the two lampstands that house the precious Light of God? The Bible indicates they would be met by a savage beast, which would overcome them. The verses read:

> And when they [the two prophets of God] shall have finished their testimony, the beast that ascendeth out of the bottomless pit shall make war against them, and shall overcome and kill them. And their dead bodies shall lie in the street of the great city which spiritually is called Sodom and Egypt, where also our Lord was crucified. And they of the peoples and kindreds and tongues and nations shall see their dead bodies three days and a half, and shall not permit their dead bodies to be put in graves. And they that dwell upon the earth shall rejoice over them, and make merry, and shall send gifts to one another, because these two prophets tormented them that dwelt upon the earth. *Revelation 11:7-10*

Muḥammad faced harsh opposition. During His lifetime, Mecca was ruled by the tribe of Quraysh, which was divided into clans. The major clan was the Hashimites, named after Háshim, Muḥammad's great-grandfather. But there were several other clans of importance, especially the Umayyads, who will become important in understanding Christian prophecy. The clans of the Quraysh, and the relationship between some of the early Muslims, have been discussed by another Bahá'í scholar.[1]

When Muḥammad publicly declared His mission, opposition from various clans of the Quraysh increased. After His declaration, He began to preach monotheism and to offer prayers both in the Ka'bah and around its courtyard. Mecca was a trading city that flourished by respecting the tribal gods of all those who came there. Muḥammad's preaching was economically dangerous to Meccans. The Quraysh took measures to stop the Prophet. Abú-Lahab, an uncle of the Prophet, began to throw trash upon Muḥammad and His followers when they were engaged in prayer. He would also scatter thorns in the places where Muḥammad and His disciples would gather.[2] As Muḥammad gained more converts, His followers were thrown into prison, starved, and beaten with sticks. Some were stripped bare and fastened to a hillside at a place called Batha, outside Mecca, where they were

1. H. M. Balyuzi, *Muhammad and the Course of Islam* (Oxford, George Ronald, 1976) p. 15.
2. Ameer 'Alí, *The Spirit of Islam*, pp. 24-26.

exposed to the intense rays of the sun and forced to recant their faith. Many did not.[3]

As Muḥammad's influence spread, the persecutions became more intense. Around the Gregorian year 615 A.D., Muḥammad bade many of His followers to escape from the city and seek refuge in the neighboring Christian kingdom of Abyssinia (Ethiopia). Eighty-three men and eighteen women took His advice, only to be pursued by agents of the Quraysh, who complained to the negus (king) of Abyssinia about Muḥammad. The king called the exiles into his presence and demanded to know more of this religion about which he had heard such abominations. Legend has it that Ja'far, brother of 'Alí, responded:

> O king, we were plunged in the depth of ignorance and barbarism; we adored idols, we lived in unchastity; we ate dead bodies, and we spoke abominations; we disregarded every feeling of humanity, and the duties of hospitality and neighbourhood; we knew no law but that of the strong, when God raised among us a man, of whose birth, truthfulness, honesty, and purity we were all aware; and he called us to the unity of God, and taught us not to associate anything with Him; he forbade us the worship of

3. If the opening of the fifth seal—which signalizes that new believers will be killed during a period of time before the Promised One comes—refers to the appearance of Islam (see Appendix 1), then, once again, history clearly reveals the prophecy was fulfilled. Hundreds of Muḥammad's early followers were put to death. Many others died in battle.

> idols; and enjoined us to speak the truth, to be faithful to our trusts, to be merciful, and to regard the rights of neighbours; he forbade us to speak evil of women, or to eat the substance of orphans; he ordered us to fly from vices, and to abstain from evil; to offer prayers, to render alms, to observe the fast. We have believed in him, we have accepted his teachings and his injunctions to worship God, and not to associate anything with Him. For this reason our people have risen against us, have persecuted us in order to make us forgo the worship of God and return to the worship of idols of wood and stone and other abominations. They have tortured us and injured us, until finding no safety among them, we have come to thy country, and hope thou will protect us from their oppression.[4]

The king responded favorably to their request.

After the agents of the Quraysh returned from Abyssinia, the enemies of Islam redoubled their efforts. Two men were particularly active in this regard: Abú-Sufyán, the leading man of the Umayyad tribe, and Abú-Jahl of the Makhzum tribe.[5] They engineered a formal treaty that stopped trading between the Quraysh and all the members of Muḥammad's clan, the Hashimites and the Muttalib. Thus, Muḥammad, His fol-

4. Ameer 'Alí, *The Spirit of Islam*, pp. 29-30.

5. Abú-Jahl is an epithet meaning "Father of Ignorance." The name was given to him by Muslims. His real name was Abu'l-Ḥakam, 'Amr Ibn Hishám.

lowers, and other non-Muslim members of these clans were forced by economic sanction to gather together in a portion of Mecca where they became virtual prisoners. Muḥammad could venture outside this area only in the months of pagan pilgrimage, when the polytheists forbade violence. During these times He began His preaching anew, but He directed it toward the traders and pilgrims visiting the ancient city.

The Flight to Medina

Eventually, under threat of assassination and with a bounty on His head, Muḥammad and His followers were forced to flee Mecca. They went to Ya<u>th</u>rib, a city several hundred miles to the north whose traders had responded favorably to Muḥammad. At about the end of June or at the beginning of July 622 A.D., Muḥammad arrived in Ya<u>th</u>rib, where some five hundred Muslim men and many women and children awaited Him. The city, which consisted of a series of fortified hamlets where the clans lived, became His. The inhabitants of the city changed its name to Madinát an-Nabí, which means "City of the Prophet"; the name was later shortened to Medínah (Medina), which means "the City."

Living in small hamlets, surrounded by enemies, Muḥammad (according to the custom of the time) organized frequent reconnaissance missions into the deserts surrounding Medina in order to guard against sudden attack. The Meccans provoked the Medinans:

they harassed villages near Medina, destroying fruit trees and stealing cattle.[6] Several brief skirmishes occurred when scouts of Meccans and scouts of Medinans caught sight of one another. Major conflict was inevitable. It finally came at the place called Badr. Under the leadership of Abú-Jahl, a man sworn to the destruction of Islam, 1,000 well-armed men set forth to do battle with a force of three hundred and fourteen ill-equipped Muslims. Muḥammad sent forth a messenger, 'Umar, with an offer of peace. The Meccans refused, though some in their ranks wavered. The small band of Muslims vanquished the army of idolaters. Abú-Jahl was killed, and seventy-four prisoners were taken.

Muḥammad began to exercise the same authority at Medina that had been given to Moses; however, He was much more merciful. Contrary to the custom of the Arabs and the injunctions found in the Old Testament, prisoners of war were not put to death. Instead, they were brought to Medina, where they were treated with kindness. One of the prisoners is reported to have said, "Blessings be on the men of Medina! They made us ride, while they themselves walked [back to Medina]; they gave us wheaten bread to eat when there was little of it; contenting themselves with dates."[7] The spiritual influence of Muḥammad on His followers was having obvious effect.

The battle of Badr was but the first of many between

6. Balyuzi, *Muḥammad and the Course of Islam*, p. 63; 'Alí, *The Spirit of Islam*, p. 6.

7. 'Alí, *The Spirit of Islam*, p. 63, note 1.

Muslims and idolaters. Because of the death of Abú-Jahl, Abú-Sufyán, the Umayyad leader, rose to prominence and swore revenge. He soon raised five-thousand men, equipped with horses and three thousand camels, to attack Muḥammad and the Medinans. The Meccans brought their women into battle to sing songs and encourage the men. In this battle the Muslim army of 1,000 men suffered near annihilation when a group of Muslim archers sensed victory was near and moved from their assigned places to gather booty. This fateful move exposed the Muslim flank and brought almost total defeat. Muḥammad, injured in battle and observing that the cause of His defeat was the waywardness of His own people, cried out, "O God, forgive my people, for they know not."

Who, then, is the beast spoken of in the biblical verses above? It is the organized opposition to Muḥammad, which later transferred its opposition to 'Alí and his descendants. This brings to the forefront the reason why the Bible indicated there are two, not one, prophet-witnesses with whom we must be concerned.

The First Rulers of Islam

Muḥammad eventually conquered Mecca and went forth to eliminate polytheism throughout Arabia. But as He lay dying, the beast of opposition arose again. This time its target was not Muḥammad, but His chosen successor. It is said that on His death bed, Muḥammad asked for writing materials so that He could dictate His last wishes.[8] Shí'í Muslims, who believe that Muḥammad had specified 'Alí to assume a spiritual station after Muḥammad's death, argue that Muḥammad wished to appoint 'Alí as His successor. They claim that Muḥammad had, on numerous occasions, indicated that 'Alí should become the leader of Islam. However, Muḥammad never put any such instructions in writing. For whatever reasons, Muḥammad did not dictate His last wishes and died without naming a clear successor. Three men succeeded Muḥammad before 'Alí took his rightful place. In the interim, elements of worldly corruption characteristic of the beast and Satan infiltrated Islam. When 'Alí was finally called to assume the leadership of Islam, the beast arose to precipitate a crisis from which Islam has never recovered.

The men who became successors to Muḥammad assumed the title "caliph" (*khalíf*), which means "deputy." They claimed no prophetic authority, yet assumed sole leadership of Islam. The first of these men was Abú-Bakr.

After Muḥammad's death, Muslims throughout Mecca debated who should succeed Him. Various Muslim groups, still harboring the very notions of tribalism which Muḥammad sought to extinguish, were anxious

8. Balyuzi, *Muhammad and the Course of Islam*, p. 153; Gibbon, *The Rise and Fall of the Roman Empire*, Vol. 3, p. 112. That Muḥammad wished to specify a successor has been questioned by Sunní apologists. A fuller account of the successorship issue can be found in Moojan Momen, *An Introduction to Shí'í Islam*, Chapter 2 (Oxford: George Ronald, 1985).

for one of their own to succeed the Prophet. The Medinan clans, who were less well-respected in Arabia than the more powerful Meccan clans, were, nevertheless, hopeful that a Medinan would succeed Muḥammad. Abú-Bakr understood that the appointing of a Medinan would be disastrous to the unity of Islam. Whether he knew of the rights of 'Alí is unclear. However, in front of an assembly of Medinans, he nominated two respected men of the Meccan Quraysh: 'Umar of the clan of 'Adí and Abú-'Ubaydah of the clan of al-Hárith. These two men refused and declared fealty on the spot to Abú-Bakr himself. This sudden turn of events met with equally sudden and near unanimous approval on the part of the Medinans, who respected Abú-Bakr. Soon thereafter, Abú-Bakr found himself the first caliph of Islam. He was from the less powerful Quraysh tribe of Banú-Taym and he was older than 'Alí, which made Him more suitable to many in that patriarchal society. A Bahá'í and Islamic scholar notes, "Abú-Bakr was a good and just ruler, a man of deep piety. But his accession to the seat of authority and the manner in which he named his successor were unrelated to any specific command of the prophet."[9]

'Alí, it appears, was not present when these events occurred and did not publicly contest the enthusiasm of the masses. To do so would have split the religion of God at a dangerous time. There still were serious external and internal threats to Islam. The Islamic nation was situated just south of the Byzantine empire, which

9. Balyuzi, *Muhammad and the Course of Islam*, p. 170.

had just defeated the Persians. False prophets also had arisen within Arabia. One named Musaylimah had begun his cult during the lifetime of the Prophet. He is said to have addressed a letter to Muḥammad which began, "From Musaylimah the messenger of God to Muḥammad messenger of God." Muḥammad replied, "From Muḥammad the messenger of God to Musaylimah the liar . . ."[10] This false prophet had grown in power and married another would-be messiah of Christian descent named Sajah. The two of them were a considerable threat to the new nation. Idolatry was not dead, and the Muslims were too new in their unity to be trusted not to return to their old ways. 'Alí wished for unity and so remained silent.

Abú-Bakr consolidated and secured many of the victories of Islam, but reigned for only two years and two months. On his death bed he appointed 'Umar to succeed him. 'Umar's reign witnessed a vast increase in the domains of Islam. Syria, Persia, and Egypt—including the important cities of Damascus and Jerusalem—were purged of polytheists and came under the rule of Islamic monotheism. Although stern, 'Umar was also conscientious of his duties to his subjects.

'Umar was assassinated by a slave in November of 644 A.D. He had ruled ten years. As he lay dying, he appointed six men as candidates to replace him. These were to choose one from among themselves. They chose

10. Montgomery W. Watt, *Muhammad, Prophet and Statesman* (Oxford: Oxford University Press, 1961) p. 225; Balyuzi *Muhammad and the Course of Islam*, p. 168.

the seventy year old ‘Uthmán. ‘Uthmán was a good man, but easily manipulated; he also was an Umayyad.

Recall that it was an Umayyad, Abú-Sufyán, who had led the Meccan forces against Muḥammad and ‘Alí while they were at Medina. Abú-Sufyán had converted to Islam only to save his skin when the Muslims were on the verge of overtaking Mecca. While the loyalty and devotion of ‘Uthmán to the unity of Islam was above reproach, the loyalty of others in his clan was not.

‘Uthmán’s great fault was that he allowed himself to be persuaded by those whose real ambition was power. In the words of Syed Ameer ‘Alí, a Shi’í apologist, “His election in the end proved the end of Islam.”[11] ‘Uthmán was inclined to favoritism, and established his relatives in positions of authority all over the Empire. He allowed his uncle, Marwan, a man whom Muḥammad himself had banished from Medina, to hold the seal of the caliph and write on his behalf. The domains of Islam continued to grow, but a completely secular dynamic appeared and grew among the administrators ‘Uthmán had chosen. Islam stretched into India and further across North Africa, but catastrophe was not far off. The Prophet Himself had foretold of a leader who would be slain by his own people because of the conflict and contention which that leader allowed to develop.[12] ‘Uthmán was that man. In June of 656 A.D., ‘Uthmán was stabbed to death while he

11. Quoted from Balyuzi, *Muhammad and the Course of Islam*, p. 174.

12. Balyuzi, *Muḥammad and the Course of Islam*, p. 176.

was reading the Qur'an. He was eighty-two years old. His rule launched Islam into a civil war from which it never recovered.

For five days the leaders consulted on whom to elect as a successor. 'Alí was chosen, Gibbon says, because he combined the qualities of a poet, a soldier, and a saint.[13] He had remained aloof from the discussions. When the delegation arrived at his house to swear loyalty to him, these were the words he spoke,

> O people! Leave me and choose someone other than me. That which faces me is an undertaking fraught with grave issues: hearts will waver, minds will falter, horizons will be dimmed, the right path will be obscured. And know this that if I respond to your call, I shall command you according to my own lights. I shall not give ear to anything which may be said, nor shall I heed any rebuke. If you pass me over and have another man to command you I shall be as one of you, and it may be that I shall listen to him and obey him more readily than you. It is better for you that I be your counsellor rather than your ruler.[14]

'Alí was displaying the same detachment that he always had. There could be no other ruler for true Muslims: The people chose him. Thus, 'Alí finally assumed the position that had been rightfully his from the begin-

13. Gibbon, *Decline and Fall of the Roman Empire*, Vol. 3, p. 119.

14. Balyuzi, *Muhammad and the Course of Islam*, p. 178.

ning. 'Alí and the three caliphs that preceded him are known by Sunní Muslims as the *rasídún*, "The Rightly-Guided Caliphs," as each of them knew the Prophet and tried to follow in His footsteps.

The Appearance of the Beast

One of 'Alí's first acts was to dismiss the corrupt governors appointed by 'Uthmán.[15] This aroused a powerful opposition group. The situation worsened when 'Alí refused to appoint two elderly, rich, and vainglorious men to the important governorships of Basrah and Kufah. Their pride and ambitions hurt, these two fled to Mecca to join forces with 'Á'ishah (a wife of Muḥammad who also had political ambitions). In Mecca, these three began to spread rumors that 'Alí had been responsible for 'Uthmán's death. Historians agree that this was untrue. The three could not stir up the people of Mecca, so they fled to Basrah to inflict damage there. In Damascus, Mu'áwíyah, the son of Abú-Sufyán, continued these rumors. As he was the ranking Umayyad, Mu'áwíyah's intentions seem clear.

Civil war broke out between Mu'áwíyah and 'Alí, and 'Alí was forced to send Muslim warrior to meet

15. The governor of Egypt, a foster-brother of 'Uthman who had been condemned to death by the Prophet Himself for interpolating the Qur'an and apostatizing, but who had been spared by 'Uthman's intervention, was one of these governors. Another was the governor of Kufa (Iraq), 'Uthman's half-brother, who had on occasion appeared drunk in public.

Muslim warrior. Balyuzi reports that even after the enemy's archers had fired at 'Alí, he was reluctant to order assaults on fellow-Muslims.[16] It is written that when one of the leaders of the opposition was beheaded by a warrior who was hoping to gain favor in the eyes of 'Alí, 'Alí wept bitterly and had the warrior driven out.[17]

More battles followed, first at Basrah and then at Siffin (north of Damascus). There, Mu'áwíyah, a master of treachery, devised a plot to rob 'Alí of his supporters. He already had gained the support of several self-seeking men by sending them letters and promising to appoint them as chiefs if he was made caliph. Now he had several of his men place the Qur'an on their spears and advance toward 'Alí's men asking for arbitration. The ruse worked. Mu'áwíyah was delighted when one of the tribes who fought under 'Alí demanded that their representative, who had once tried to mobilize people against 'Alí, be appointed arbitrator. The arbitrator chosen by the tribe was easily manipulated by the crafty arbitrator of Mu'áwíyah. Mu'áwíyah's man, began by convincing 'Alí's arbitrator that both 'Alí and Mu'áwíyah should cease their claims to the caliphate while the matter was discussed. 'Alí's undeputized arbitrator was made to take off his ring and publicly declare that he renounced the caliphate of 'Alí. Mu'áwíyah's deputy was supposed to

16. Balyuzi, *Muḥammad and the Course of Islam*, p. 181.
17. The beheaded man was az-Zubayr, who opposed 'Alí because he wanted a governorship.

do the same thing. Instead, he put on the other arbitrator's ring and declared Mu'áwíyah the new caliph. Pandemonium ensued, and 'Alí and his confused men retreated to Kúfah by the Euphrates.

On January 27, 661 A.D., a deranged assassin took the life of 'Alí. Three men had plotted to kill those whom they considered the source of Islam's problems: 'Alí, Mu'áwíyah, and 'Amr (Mu'áwíyah's arbitrator). Mu'áwíyah was wounded, and 'Amr escaped when his assassin attacked the wrong man; only 'Alí was killed. Mu'áwíyah, his Umayyad enemy, became caliph. Mu'áwíyah's character is revealed by his practice of fabricating traditions which he ascribed to Muḥammad to ensure that he obtained what he wanted. He also instituted ritual cursing of 'Alí from the pulpit.[18] Gibbon wrote of the takeover by the Umayyads of the leadership of Islam.

> The persecutors of Muhammad usurped the inheritance of his children; and the champions of idolatry became the supreme heads of his religion and empire.[19]

Thus it came true, as the Book of Revelation foretold, that a beast attacked and eventually defeated the two prophet-witnesses of Islam. In the language of prophecy, these two witnesses of God were killed and "the

18. Balyuzi, *Muḥammad and the Course of Islam*, p. 191-192.
19. Gibbon, *The Decline and Fall of the Roman Empire*, Vol. 3, p. 124.

peoples and kindreds, and tongues, and nations . . . shall not permit their dead bodies to be put in graves." That is, the religion of Muḥammad and 'Alí was dishonored by the Muslims that joined the ranks of their enemies. Without the spirit of Muḥammad and 'Alí, the body of Islam would become just another secular empire, exposed and open to the world's ridicule.

But this is not the end of the prophesy, for we in the West are represented in it as well. The verses say: "And they that dwell upon the earth shall rejoice over them . . . because these two prophets tormented them that dwelt upon the earth." Do we in the West not rejoice in the set backs that Islam (and especially Shí'í Islam) experiences?

The story of the two prophet-witnesses of Islam does not end here, however. The biblical theme continues.

The Return in Three and a Half Days

It is a common theme in the Bible for a spiritual leader to claim to be another long dead, and for people to expect the return of a past prophet. Consider how Jesus conferred upon John the Baptist the station of the returned Elijah, and how Christ is seen to be with Moses and Elijah on the mount of transfiguration. So it should be easy to understand that the two prophet-witnesses spoken of in the following verses are actually different people returning in the spirit of Muḥammad and 'Alí, to complete their work. The verses read:

> And after three days and a half the spirit of life from God entered them [the two witnesses], and they stood upon their feet, and a great fear fell upon them who saw them. And they heard a great voice from heaven saying unto them, Come up here. And they ascended up to heaven in a cloud, and their enemies beheld them. *Revelation 11:11-12*

Let us now look at the time period specified in the verses. We already have seen how the Bible allows us to interpret days as years. Thus, the three and a half days, may be understood as three and a half years, which is 1,260 days. Now we are back at a familiar symbol: forty-two months, or 1,260 days. And, as we saw earlier, that is the length (in years) of the dispensation of Islam. This application of the principle of a year for a day and a day for a year should not be surprising: The Bible has done both.[20]

20. Numbers 14:34 converts days to years: "After the number of the days in which ye searched the land, even forty days, each day for a year, shall ye bear your iniquities, even forty years, and ye shall know my breach of promise." The verses of Ezekiel 4:6 ff converts these years of iniquity back to days: "Lie also upon thy left side, and lay the iniquity of the house of Israel upon it; according to the number of the days thou shalt lie upon it, thou shalt bear their iniquity. For I have laid upon thee the years of their iniquity, according to the number of days, three hundred and ninety days, so shalt thou bear the iniquity of the house of Israel. And when thou hast accomplished them [the years of iniquity], lie again on

The Trumpet Blast of the Seventh Angel

The Muslim year 1260 A.H. is the Christian year 1844 A.D. I will not speak yet of the specifics of what happened in that year, but it is the date of the beginning of the second woe and the dawn of the return of the two witnesses. But the Book of Revelation indicates that what happens after this date is even more important:

> And the same hour was there a great earthquake, and the tenth part of the city fell, and in the earthquake were slain of men seven thousand; and the remnant were terrified, and gave glory to God of heaven. The second woe is past and, behold, the third woe cometh quickly. And the seventh angel sounded; and there were great voices in heaven, saying, The kingdom of this world is become the kingdom of our Lord, and of his Christ, and he shall reign forever and ever. And the four and twenty elders, who sat before God on their thrones, fell upon their faces, and worshiped God, Saying, We give thee thanks, O Lord God Almighty, who art, and wast, and art to come, because thou hast taken to thee thy great power, and hast reigned. And the nations were angry and thy wrath is come,

thy right side, and thou shalt bear the iniquity of the house of Judah forty days; I have appointed thee each day for a year."

> and the time of the dead, that they should be judged, and that thou shouldest give reward unto thy servants, the prophets, and to the saints, and them that fear thy name, small and great, and shouldest destroy them who destroy the earth. And the temple of God was opened in heaven, and there was seen in his temple the ark of his covenant; and there were lightnings, and voices, and thunderclaps, and an earthquake, and great hail. *Revelation 11:13-19*

The victory comes after the second woe, as the seventh Angel sounds His trumpet. This victory and trumpet blast is the Revelation from God that is associated with both the judgment and the establishment of Christ's kingdom on earth. We will return to this theme later.

THE SEVEN TRUMPET BLASTS
(*Revelation 8:1-13 and 9:1-21*)

Chapter 7

THE TWELVE STARS OF THE FIRST ADVENT

As we have discussed, the ministry of the fifth trumpet blast, the first advent of a prophet of God after Jesus, was comprised of two prophet-witnesses and lasted for 1,260 days, which we know to be 1,260 years. After these 1,260 years, the Bible states that there will be a return of the two witnesses. This return will be the sixth trumpet blast, the second woe, which will be followed shortly by the appearance of the third and final woe. This theme that three Messengers of God will come after the time of Jesus is so important that the Bible now returns to tell the story again. This time more detail is added and a different set of symbols is employed.

What if the second Messenger of God after Jesus came from the literal and spiritual descendents of the first Messenger after Jesus? This is the reality which Chapter twelve of the Book of Revelation sets out to explain. Once again, the chief characters are Muḥammad and 'Alí, and more detail of the history of Islam will be added. But this time special emphasis will be placed upon their descendents.

Chapter 12 begins:

> And there appeared a great wonder in heaven—a woman clothed with the sun, and the moon under her feet, and upon her head a crown of twelve stars. And she being with child, cried, travailing in birth, and pained to be delivered. *Revelation 12:1-2*

The Work of Islam

The woman has been interpreted by Christian scholars in many ways.[1] But it is important to see the vision in perspective. The woman gives birth to one who apparently is the Messiah: "a male child, who was to rule all nations with a rod of iron."[2] But the dragon, Satan, appears to devour the child, and the woman is forced to flee into the wilderness for 1,260 days. At the end of this time, we assume, the earth will receive the child. The interpretation then must explain the identities of the woman, the Messiah, the dragon, why the analogy

1. The woman is often seen as the idealized Messianic community, the ideal Israel from which the Messiah would come (See Beckwith, *The Apocalypse of John* and Mounce, *Commentary on the New Testament: The Book of Revelation*). However, the Messiah here is not Jesus. Interpretations that make the woman equal to the Israel from which Jesus came and the son equal to Jesus rob the verses of their prophetic significance and are vigorously rejected by many Christian scholars. The verses, in the time they were written, refer to the future, not the past.
2. *Revelation 12:5.*

of birth is used, and the significance of the length of time. All of this is easy to understand, if we take Islam into account.

The woman who is laboring to deliver her child Messiah symbolizes the work of religion, the spiritual will or law of God which needs to be accomplished.[3] In each religious dispensation, there is a work to be accomplished, a law to be established, hearts to win, and minds to educate. However, there is one special work that the woman of Islam must perform: She must give birth to the Messiah. So the significance of the work of Muḥammad and 'Alí is not just that they brought forth another religion. It is that from their progeny would come the Promised One. This is why the analogy of birth is used. We turn now to consider the descendents of Muḥammad, to those who oppossed them, and to the length of time before the Messiah's birth.

The Twelve Imams

The woman in the prophecy has a crown of twelve stars. The twelve stars have been interpreted as the twelve tribes and as the twelve disciples of Jesus. But these interpretations miss the prophetic significance of the verses. It is the Second Coming with which we are concerned, not the first. The twelve stars are the twelve

3. "This woman [in Revelation 12] is that bride [spoken of in Revelation 21], the Law of God that descended upon Muhammad." 'Abdu'l-Bahá , *Some Answered Questions*, p. 68

Imams of Islam. The daughter of Muḥammad, Fáṭimah, was married to ‘Alí. The offspring of this union have vast prophetic significance in the Bible and in history and are the reason why it is important to consider both the work of Muḥammad and ‘Alí in interpreting scripture. It is the reason the Bible spoke of the work of *two* prophet-witnesses in Islam. The first twelve male lineal descendents from ‘Alí and Fáṭimah are known in Shí'ih Islam as the Twelve Imams.[4] These are the twelve stars that were upon the head of the woman, from which the Promised One would come. These also may be the twelve princes whom God had in mind when He blessed Ishmael in the Book of Genesis.[5] The historian Gibbon writes of the twelve Imams:[6]

4. The branch of Shí'ih Islam that believes them to have a special station is known as "Twelver Islam." The title "Imam" originates from the word "imam" which means "the one who stands in front." It refers to the one who leads the congregational prayer in the mosque, which ‘Alí often did. According to Shí'ih Islam, it was the intention of Muḥammad to appoint a successor, ‘Alí, with a spiritual station. Shí'is are divided upon what was to happen upon the death of ‘Alí. However, the transfer of the Imamate via the descendents of ‘Alí was a common thought. The Twelvers represent one branch of Shí'í thought.

5. "And as for Ishmael, I have heard thee: behold, I have blessed him, and will make him fruitful, and will multiply him exceedingly; twelve princes shall he beget, and I will make him a great nation." *Genesis 17:20.* The listing of twelve sons (princes) of Ishmael in *Genesis 25:13-16*, may have been an attempt to close the promise prematurely.

6. It is unclear if the eleventh Imam had a son. As knowledge of a son would have put the child's life in danger, it is easy to

> [T]hese royal saints despised the pomp of the world; submitted to the will of God and the injustice of man; and devoted their innocent lives to the study and practice of their religion. The twelfth and last of the Imams, conspicuous by the title of Mahadi, or the Guide, surpassed the solitude and sanctity of his predecessors. He concealed himself in a cavern near Bagdad: the time and place of his death are unknown; and his votaries pretend that he still lives, and will appear before the day of judgement to overthrow the tyranny of Dejal, or the Antichrist.[7]

The Dragon That Casts Down Stars

The next symbol we must interpret is the dragon waiting to devour the child Messiah:

> And there appeared a great red dragon having seven heads and ten horns, and seven crowns upon his heads. And his tail drew the third part of the stars of heaven and cast them to the earth; and the dragon stood before the woman who was ready to be delivered, to

understand why the existence of a son may have been obscurred. Conversely, if there was no son, one may have been invented to keep the line of descent alive. Followers of Twelver Islam believe the eleventh Imam had a son. This is the tradition Gibbon sites.

7. Gibbon, *The Rise and Fall of the Roman Empire*, Vol. 3. pp. 127-128.

> devour her child as soon as it was born. *Revelation 12:3-4*

The dragon, we are told, is a symbol for the "devil and Satan, who deceiveth the whole world."[8] It is the embodiment of the spirit of evil, which feeds the base desires of humans, and which opposses God's agents. But the work of the dragon is very specific. It is to make war with the descendents of Muḥammad and 'Alí and thus, to kill those from whom the Promised One will come.

The Umayyad leaders, who became the heads of the Islamic empire, were only vulnerable as leaders of Islam when their spiritual leadership was challenged. The natural champions of alternative leadership of Islam came from the descendents of Muḥammad and 'Alí. Any one of these descendents could claim to be the true leader of Islam at any moment. Fearing a messianic uprising within Islam, the Umayyad leaders watched these holy descendents of Muḥammad and 'Alí for any sign of revolt. They killed any of them who threatened their power.

In the language of prophecy, there were seven heads to the dragon of the Umayyad empire. In this case, a head is a region of the Islamic empire. While it is possible to demarcate seven regions in the Empire, it is unnecessary.[9] Seven is simply a symbol of complete-

8. *Revelation 12:9.*

9. It makes little difference how you divide the pie of the Old World, but in Bahá'í writings it has been divided into seven domin-

ness. Thus, the holy descendents were persecuted throughout the Islamic domain. The ten horns are the ten names of the Umayyad leaders from Abú-Sufáyn to the last Umayyad, Marwán.[10] It is unnecessary to prove that all these leaders were bad men. Some, in fact, notably 'Umar, may have done good.[11] However, their leadership was not the correct leadership of Islam, and they held power at the expense of the true leaders: the descendents of Muḥammad and 'Alí.

While some of the Imams were able, for awhile, to live quiet lives, all were threatened and many were killed. Thus it occurred, as the Bible had foretold, that "the third part of the stars of heaven"—the Imams of early Islam were killed and "cast . . . to the earth." It is impossible to tell if exactly a third part, i.e. four, of

ions: "The *Roman dominion around Damascus*, and the *Persian*, *Arabian*, and *Egyptian* dominions, together with the *dominion of Africa*, that is to say Tunis, Morocco, and Algeria, the *dominion of Andulsia* which is now Spain, and the *dominion of Turkestan and Transoxania*. The Bani-Umayya had power over these countries." 'Abdú'l-Bahá, *Some Answered Questions*, p. 69. (Emphasis mine.)

10. The ten names are: Abú-Sufáyn, Mu'áwíyah, Yazíd, Marwan, 'Abdu'l-Malik, Al-Walíd, Sulaymán, 'Umar, Hishim, Ibráhim. There are 15 Umayyad leaders (Abú-Sufáyn as progenitor and 14 Umayyad caliphs descended from him). However, repetitive names (e.g., Mu'áwíyah II, Yazíd II, Yazíd III, Al-Walíd II, and Marwán II) are not counted in the prophecy. It is the names which are the horns, not the people ('Abdu'l-Bahá, *Some Answered Questions*, pp. 69-70). Ten also is merely a symbol of completeness.

11. 'Umar ended the ritual cursing of 'Alí and reintroduced more of a spiritual dimension into Islam. See Balyuzi, *Muḥammad and the Course of Islam*, p. 209.

the Imams were killed. It may have been four or more that were killed. Also, the prophecy might not have meant to identify the precise number. In either case, the spirit of the prophecy was fulfilled. The dragon, it seems, had won. But only for awhile.

The Hijrah

The next verses speak of the birth of the Messiah, but only after a long delay precipitated by the work of the dragon:

> And she brought forth a male child, who was to rule all nations with a rod of iron; and her child was caught up unto God, and to his throne. And the woman fled into the wilderness, where she hath a place prepared by God, that they should feed her there a thousand two hundred and threescore days. *Revelation 12:5-6*

Our task is to identify the beginning and ending places for the 1,260 "days" (years). The verses above, and a parallel verse (Revelation 12:14), fix the beginning of this period with the flight of the woman into the wilderness. The Islamic calendar begins with Muḥammad's flight (Hijrah) from Mecca to Medina. The spirit of true religion—in symbolic terms, a woman being pursued by a dragon—fled into the wilderness of the

Hijaz. Muḥammad and 'Alí fled from the dragon of the Umayyads. The date of this flight was the Christian year 622. It became year 1 of the Muslim Calendar, A.H. (after the Hijrah). Exactly 1,260 years later, the male child born to rule all nations would appear.

Michael and Islam

The next verses introduce the archangel Michael doing battle with the dragon:

> And there was war in heaven; Michael and his angels fought against the dragon, and the dragon fought and his angels, And prevailed not, neither was their place found any more in heaven. And the great dragon was cast out, that old serpent, called the Devil and Satan, who deceiveth the whole world; he was cast out into the earth, and his angels were cast out with him. And I heard a loud voice saying in heaven, Now is come salvation, and strength, and the kingdom of our God, and the power of his Christ; for the accuser of our brethren is cast down, who accused them before our God day and night. And they overcame him by the blood of the Lamb, and by the word of their testimony; and they loved not their lives unto the death. Therefore rejoice, ye heavens, and ye that dwell in them. Woe to the

> inhabiters of the earth and of the sea! For the devil is come down unto you, having great wrath, because he knoweth that he hath but a short time. *Revelation 12:7-12*

It is unclear if these verses refer to the battle at the beginning of the 1,260 days or to the times at the end of the 1,260 days. If the text refers to the former, Michael symbolizes the protector of the holy community, in this case true Islam. Both the angels Gabriel and Michael are quranic figures and are not the exclusive property of Israel. The Qur'an reads, "Whosoever is an enemy to God and His angels and His Messengers, and Gabriel and Michael—surely God is an enemy to the unbelievers."[12] In fact, Muslims hold that it was the angel Gabriel who brought the Revelation of God to Muḥammad.[13] Michael also may be considered the protector of the religious community of true Islam.

The verses, however, may refer to the time at the end of the 1,260 days. The Book of Daniel supports the latter interpretation. Michael appears at the end times, at the brink of great destruction, to rescue Israel.[14] In this

12. *Surah 2:98.*

13. The source of this may be Surah 2:97: "Say, Whosoever is an enemy to Gabriel—he it was that brought it down upon thy [Muḥammad's] heart by the leave of God, confirming what was before it, and for a guidance and good tidings to the believers."

14. Daniel 12:1 introduces Michael and reads, "And at that time shall Michael stand up, the great prince who standeth for the children of thy people, and there shall be a time of trouble, such as never was since there was a nation even to that same time; and at

case, the verses would refer to a future restoration of Israel to occur after 1,260 years. As we will explain, this began in the Muslim year 1260.

Having the Testimony of Christ

The last verses of Revelation 12 retell the story of the woman charged with giving birth to the Islamic Messiah, having to flee into the wilderness for "time, times and half a time." As a time is a year, this is the three and a half years, or 1,260 days, with which we are so familiar. The verses read:

> And when the dragon saw that he was cast unto the earth, he persecuted the woman who brought forth the male child. And to the woman were given two wings of a great eagle, that she might fly into the wilderness, into her place, where she is nourished for a time, and

---

that time thy people shall be delivered, every one that shall be found written in the book." The question is, at what time is Michael doing his work? It appears from Daniel 12:6-7 it is at the end of the 1,260 days: "And one said to the man clothed in linen, who was above the waters of the river, *How long shall it be to the end of these wonders?* And I heard the man clothed in linen who was above the waters of the river, when he held up his right hand unto heaven, and swore by him who liveth forever, that *it shall be for a time, times, and a half*; and when he shall have accomplished the breaking up of the power of the holy people, all these things shall be finished." (Italics mine) The end of these wonders would be at the end of 1,260 years.

> times, and half a time, from the face of the serpent. And the serpent cast out of his mouth water like a flood after the woman, that he might cause her to be carried away by the flood. And the earth helped the woman, and the earth opened her mouth and swallowed up the flood which the dragon cast out of his mouth. And the dragon was angry with the woman, and went to make war with the remnant of her seed, who keep the commandments of God, and have the testimony of Jesus Christ. *Revelation 12:13-17*

During these days (which are years), the descendents of Muḥammad and 'Alí (the remnant of the woman's seed, who were to complete Islam) were persecuted. These were the souls who kept the commandments of God and had the testimony of Jesus Christ. Note, this last verse does not say that the early Muslims were Christians. It says they had the testimony of Christ. This they had in two ways: They continued the testimony of Christ by bringing both the stories of Old and New Testaments to Muslims and by continuing the prophetic hope of Christianity and Islam to a common fulfillment through the descendents of Muḥammad and 'Alí.[15] Secondly, if the early believers of Islam are,

15. Westerners should note that the Qur'an retells many of the stories of Old and New Testament. Muḥammad thereby validated these religions to the Muslim world.

indeed, referred to in this prophecy, then, by virtue of being mentioned in this prophecy, they had the testimony of Christ. Christ is the author of the prophecy.[16]

16. This argument is not as cyclical as it may sound. The statement that Christ testified for these people, and that these people may be Muslims, may provide the necessary impetus for Christians to reevaluate Islam.

DANIEL'S VISION
of four great beasts. (*Daniel 7:1-18*)

Chapter 8

THE DAYS OF DANIEL

Before we consider the second Messenger of God after Jesus who, as I have noted, appeared in the year 1844 A.D., I should note that many Christians expected the Lord to return in that same year. In this chapter I will explain how some of them identified the year 1844 as the time for the advent of the Lord.

As the year 1844 approached, a substantial messianic movement began in the West. William Miller, a champion of this cause in New England, wrote: "Wolff of Asia [Palestine]; Irwin, late of England, Mason of Scotland; Davis of South Carolina; and quite a number in this region are, or, have given the cry."[1] Others too were involved: Leonard Kelber in Germany; Edward Irving in England; and Harriet Livermore, who warned the U.S. House of Representatives, spoke often of Christ's imminent return.[2] So great was the cry that an English clergyman wrote:

1. *Evidence from Scripture and History of the Second Coming of Christ about the Year 1843*, Lecture 16 (Boston: Joshua V. Hines) p. 238.

2. Henry James Forman mentions these names in, *The Story of Prophecy* (London: Cassell and Company Ltd., 1936).

> It is not merely in Great Britain that the expectation of the near return of the Redeemer is entertained, and the voice of warning raised, but also in America, India, and on the continent of Europe. In America about three hundred ministers of the Word are thus preaching this gospel of the kingdom; whilst in this country, about seven hundred of the Church of England are raising the same cry.[3]

These ministers were given signs in the heavens to consider as well. In 1833 there had been a fantastic falling-star shower. The signs, if they were signs, continued. In 1843 a comet appeared with a tail that stretched 108 million miles into the heavens, and in that same year, a very unusual halo appeared around the sun.[4] Public expectation grew. Another writer, looking back on this era, summed up: "The causes for religious stirrings were at that period in the air and ubiquitous."[5]

Mostly unaware that the year 1844 was also the Muslim year 1260, the Adventists and others huddled in anxious anticipation of the advent of the Lord.[6] How

3. *New York Tribune*, November 20, 1838.

4. These signs are given by Forman, *The Story of Prophecy*, 1936.

5. Forman, *The Story of Prophecy*, 1936, p. 310.

6. The significance of the connection had been realized by some. The Christian scholar H. Grattan Guinness had written, "This is the more remarkable also as this [1844 A.D.] is the 1260th year of the Hegira." *The Approaching End of the Age* (London: Hodder and Stoughton, 1880) p. 438.

had they chosen 1844 as the focus of their hopes? There is no one answer to the question. Some realized that Christ's gospel had been spread throughout the world, and felt that a precondition for the Return set forth in the Bible had been met.[7] Many simply saw that the signs of the times indicated the nearness of the Lord. But some were convinced by prophecies in the Book of Daniel that had spoken, not only of the coming of Jesus, but also of the date of the end times.

Seven Times Till the Most High Rules

According to Biblical scholars, Daniel the prophet was carried off to Babylon after the first siege and capture of Jerusalem, sometime around 606 or 605 B.C.[8] In Babylon, King Nebuchadnezzar soon became aware of Daniel's wisdom and skill in interpreting dreams, and Daniel became an adviser to the king. According to the Bible (Daniel 2:1): "In the second year of the reign of

7. This refers to *Matthew 24:14*: "And this gospel of the kingdom shall be preached in all the world for a witness unto all nations; and then shall the end come."

8. Scholars disagree on the dates. After a reasoned review, J. F. Walvoord concludes that "the third year of Jehoiakim, king of Judah," in which, according to Daniel, "Nebuchadnezzar, king of Babylon, [entered] unto Jerusalem, and besieged it" and which would also mark the beginning of Daniel's captivity was the summer of 605 B.C. (*Daniel: the Key to Prophetic Revelation* [Chicago: Moody Press, 1971].) Other estimates range from 604 to 607 B.C.

Nebuchadnezzar, Nebuchadnezzar dreamed dreams, and his spirit was troubled, and his sleep went from him." This would have been in the year 602.[9] The king summoned Daniel and others to help interpret his dreams. Only Daniel was successful.

Nebuchadnezzar's first dream was of a great image whose head was gold, breast and arms were silver, belly and thighs were bronze, legs were iron, and feet were iron and clay. In the dream, a great stone cut from a mountain struck the image on the feet and the entire statue crumbled and was scattered in the wind. The stone remained, becoming a great mountain filling the whole earth. Daniel informed the king that he was the head of gold, and that the other parts of the image were kingdoms which would arise after his. As to the stone, we are told that "in the days of these kings [those of iron and clay] shall the God of heaven set up a kingdom, which shall never be destroyed."[10] This new kingdom would "consume all kingdoms."

The Bible does not provide the key to the other parts of the image, only the head. Consequently, interpretations vary. But if we consider the major kingdoms which followed Babylonia, we may interpret the silver

9. Nebuchadnezzar became king in 605, soon after the capture of Jerusalem and the death of his father. However, Walvoord and others note, in Babylonian reckoning, the first year of a king is known as "the year of accession." The next year then becomes the first year of his reign. Thus, three years pass before the second year of Nebuchadnezzar's reign, when the dreams begin. The year would be 602.

10. *Daniel 2:44.*

breast and arms as the Medes and the Persians, the bronze belly and thighs as the Greeks, the iron legs the Romans, and the many kingdoms which appeared, like toes, out of the Roman Empire, as the feet of iron and clay. The next great kingdom, the one from God, would be that foretold by Christ (for example, in the Lord's prayer), promised again by Muḥammad, and at last brought to fruition in our day.

It is Nebuchadnezzar's second dream, however, that supplies us with the date for the arrival of that Promised Kingdom. This dream was of a great tree that was hewn down. The stump was left in the fields, its roots tethered with an iron and bronze ring, and the heart of the stump was to be changed to a beast's heart for seven times (years). The king, Daniel explained, was the tree that would fall. He would be driven into the fields for seven years.

This prophecy has two fulfillments: The Bible says that Nebuchadnezzar was driven out of his kingdom and that he roamed mad, as a beast in the field, for seven years.[11] There is, however, another more important fulfillment that refers to the time when the Lord's Kingdom will finally be established on earth. The verse which introduces this interpretation reads:

> This matter [of the seven years] is by the decree of the watchers, and the demand by the word of the holy ones, to the intent that

11. The historical evidence for this interpretation is not substantial.

> the living may know that *the Most High ruleth in the kingdom of men*, and giveth it to whomsoever he will, and setteth up over it the basest [most humble] of men. *Daniel 4:17* (Emphasis mine.)

This is what Christians pray for: that the Lord's Kingdom be established *on earth*, in the kingdom of man, as it is in heaven. When was this to happen? In seven times. As we've discussed, a *time* is a biblical way of saying a *year*. Thus, we are promised the kingdom will be established in seven years. Using the Biblical reckoning of a day for a year, these seven years represent 2,520 days, each of which may be a year.[12] Thus, if Nebuchadnezzar had his dream in 602 B.C., we may count forward 2,520 years. But on which calendar? If we use the Hebrew or Babylonian calendars, both of which use lunar years of 354 days, we arrive at 892,080 days. If we then divide by 365 days (as in our calendar), we arrive at 2,444 years. Beginning at 602 B.C. and moving forward 2,444 years, we arrive at 1842/43.[13] If the advent cannot occur until *after* the full seven years pass,

12. Recall that the practice of counting days as years is old and supported by the Bible itself. See, for example, Numbers 14:34 and Ezekiel 4:6. In prophecy, it is common to assume that a month has 30 days, and thus a year has 360 days. This is based on Genesis 7 and 8, in which months are given 30 days in God's time. Thus, 7 years x 360 days = 2,520 days.

13. The Hebrew civil calendar runs from September-October to September-October. The Hebrew religious year begins in March-April. Thus, it takes a split year to define it in our terms.

then the first year in which God's kingdom on earth can be established is the year 1844.[14]

The Adventists and Daniel

This prophecy is only the first in the Book of Daniel that points to the year 1844. The entire book is oriented in this way, and this fact partly explains the millennial excitement that occurred around the year 1844. In 1944 (the one hundredth anniversary of their dramatic predictions that the Lord would come in 1844) one group of Adventists published a detailed account of their reckoning of prophecy. The book, *The Prophecies of Daniel and Revelation* by Uriah Smith, serves as reference for this next section.[15]

In Chapter eight of the Book of Daniel, Daniel him-

14. Neither I, nor anyone else, knows if what I have proposed is the correct way to translate the time specified (2,520 years) into calendar time. Other, more complicated, translations are certainly possible, but are arguably no better than the one I have proposed. Actually, I am amazed that any translation arrives at the year 1844, and I take it as a proof of the translation method when it can arrive at that auspicious year, especially by so straightforward a reckoning. It may be important to note that 2,520 years can be divided into two equal intervals of 1,260 years. Thus we must consider the possibility that some biblical references to 1,260 days (which are years) may relate to the first interval of time which ended with the appearance of Muḥammad.

15. Uriah Smith, *The Prophecies of Daniel and the Revelation*, (Washington, D.C.: Review and Herald Publishing Association, 1944).

self has a vision, in which he sees a goat attack and beat a ram.[16] The Book of Daniel identifies the goat as Greece and the two-horned ram as the Medes and the Persians. The Greek goat had one great horn, which broke as he became very strong. Then four new horns appeared. Interpreters say that the horn represents Alexander's Empire, and the four smaller horns are the four kingdoms that arose after Alexander's death.[17] Scripture states:

> And out of one of them came forth *a little horn*, which grew exceedingly great, toward the south, and toward the east, and toward the pleasant land. And it grew great, even to the hosts of heaven; and it *cast down some of the stars to the ground* and stamped upon them. Yea, he magnified himself even to the prince of the hosts, and by him the daily sacrifice was taken away, and the place of his sanctuary was cast down. *Daniel 8:9-11* (Emphasis mine.)

16. The date of the vision in chapter 8, is given as "in the third year of the King Belshazzar." This has been dated as 551 B.C. by John F. Walvoord (*Daniel: The Key to Prophetic Revelation*, 1971). It is believed Daniel may have lived till 530 B.C.

17. When Alexander died, his kingdom was broken into four parts and distributed among his generals. Cassander ruled Macedonia, Seleusus ruled Syria; Ptolemy ruled Egypt; and Lysimachus ruled Thrace and Asia Minor.

That "little horn" that arose out of one of the four horns has been identified by Bible scholars as the Seleucid king of Syria, Antiochus IV (Epiphanes).[18] In 168 B.C. he sent 20,000 troops to Jerusalem and massacred many of the Jewish Pietists. Thus, in the symbols of prophecy, he cast some of the star-like leaders to the ground.[19] A short time later he suspended the ritual temple sacrifice, and placed pagan images upon the altar of the temple.[20]

However, interpreting the last part of this vision has been much more difficult. The verses read:

> Then I heard one saint speaking, and another saint said unto that certain saint who spoke, "How long shall be the vision concerning the daily sacrifice, and the transgression of desolation, to give both the sanctuary and the host to be trampled underfoot?" And he said unto me, "*Unto two thousand and three hundred days; then shall the sanctuary be cleansed.*" *Daniel 8:13-14* (Emphasis mine.)

18. See Beckwith, *The Apocalypse of John*, pp. 178-181. Also, *The New English Bible with the Apocrypha: Oxford Study Edition* (Oxford: Oxford University Press, 1976). See note to *Daniel 8:9.*

19. The date comes from Chaim Potok, *Wanderings* (New York: Alfred A. Knopf, 1978) pp. 187-188.

20. According to Potok, the decree to stop loyalty to the Torah was given between April and December, 167 B.C. *The New English Bible* (notes to 1 Maccabbees 1:54) sets it at December 7, 167. It

Some have attempted to prove that the prophecy was fulfilled during the reign of Antiochus IV. However, the dates do not fit. The temple was desecrated in December of 167 B.C. It was rededicated after the death of Antiochus IV, in December of 164, three years later.[21] Twenty-three hundred days (6.39 years) after it was desecrated, in the year 160, nothing spectacular happened. However, in an attempt to make history fit the prophecy, some Christian interpreters began to look for other beginning and ending points. The most common attempt was to use the assassination of the high priest Onias III in 171 as the beginning point, and the death of Antiochus in 164 as the end. Not only does this disregard the obvious beginning and ending places of desecration and rededication, if a historical interpretation is correct, it also is imprecise. As one Christian scholar writes: "The evidence available today does not offer fulfillment to the precise day."[22] In short, the 2,300 days don't fit. Nor should they. Even after the rededication of the temple, the Jews were involved in a complex guerrilla war with their Syrian masters that lasted until 142 B.C., twenty-six years after the temple

may be worthwhile to note that the arch enemy of Muḥammad and 'Alí, Mu'áwíyah, set up his capital in Syria as well. Thus we may think of the prophecy as having two fulfillments.

21. Both dates of desecration and rededication are taken from the footnotes to 1 Maccabees of the Oxford Study Edition of the New English Bible.

22. John F. Walvoord, *Daniel, the Key to Prophetic Revelation*, p. 190.

had been desecrated.[23] The 2,300 days refer neither to literal days nor to events associated with Antiochus. The prophecy is an end-time vision and, as we shall see, the author has in mind another starting point.

The Adventists correctly understood this. They realized that the ritual cleansing of the temple occurred, according to scripture, only once a year.[24] On this day, the only day when the high priest was allowed in the inner sanctuary of the temple, the priest offered an atonement for the sins of Israel.[25] This day is known as the Day of Atonement, or Yom Kippur. Accordingly, the Adventists and others realized that the days in the prophecy referred to years. 2,300 days of atonement equalled 2,300 years of atonement.[26]

The author of the scripture specifies the correct starting point of the 2,300 days in the verses that follow. These explain the identity of the ram and the goat. Then a new prophecy is introduced. The verses read:

23. In 142 B.C., the Jews were acknowledged as independent and exempted from paying tribute by Demetrius II, king of Syria (Potok, *Wanderings*, p. 189).

24. *Leviticus 16:29.*

25. See *Exodus 30:10*, *Hebrews 9:7-8*, and *Leviticus 16:30.*

26. The verse translated here in the King James Bible as 2,300 days, is translated elsewhere as 2,300 evenings and mornings. (See, for example, *The New English Bible.*) There has been some attempt to render these evenings and mornings other than 2,300 days. However, the Christian commentator C. F. Keil writes, "A Hebrew reader could not possibly understand the period of 2300 evening-mornings of 2300 half-days or 1150 whole days, because evening and morning at the creation constituted not the half but

> And *in the latter time of their kingdom*, when transgressors are come to the full, *a king of fierce countenance, and understanding dark sentences*, shall stand up. And his power shall be mighty, but not by his own power; and he shall prosper, and continue, and shall destroy the mighty and holy people. And through his policy also he shall cause deceit to prosper in his hand; and he shall magnify himself in his heart, and by peace shall destroy many; *he shall also stand up against the Prince of princes*, but he shall be broken without hand. *Daniel 8:23-25* (Emphasis mine.)

These verses, the Adventists and others believe, refer not to the Greek Syrians, but to a kingdom which arose *in the latter times* of the Greeks, after the Greek kingdom had fallen. This new kingdom was the Roman Empire. It was the Romans who spoke a language ("*dark sentences*") which the Jews, many of whom spoke Greek, did not understand. It was also a Roman ruler who stood up against the *Prince of princes*, Jesus, but did not prevail.

---

the whole day. Still less, in the designation of time, 'till 2300 evening-mornings,' could 'evening-mornings' be understood as of the evening and morning sacrifices, and the words be regarded as meaning that till 1150 evening sacrifices and 1150 morning sacrifices are discontinued. We must therefore take the words as they are, i.e., understanding them as 2300 whole days." *Biblical Commentary on the Book of Daniel* (Eerdmans, 1955) p. 304.

Scripture tells us that Daniel did not understand this vision. But sometime later, while he was at prayer, the angel Gabriel appeared, "to give [Daniel] skill and understanding" of the dream.[27] Gabriel explained:

> *Seventy weeks are determined upon thy people and upon thy holy city*, to finish the transgression, and to make an end of sins, and to bring in everlasting righteousness, and to seal up the vision and the prophecies, *and to anoint the most Holy. Daniel 9:24* (Emphasis mine.)

The English translation "weeks" above actually is a poor choice for the Hebrew word "shabua" which is simply the plural of seven. Whether the sevens are days, weeks, months, or years is unspecified. The Adventists realized that the seventy sevens was "cut off" (a better translation of the word "determined") from the 2,300 days of the previous vision.

The next verse indicates the beginning point for both prophecies:

> Know therefore, and understand, that *from the going forth of the commandment* to restore and to build Jerusalem unto the Messiah, the Prince, shall be seven weeks, and

27. *Daniel 9:22-24.*

> threescore and two weeks; the street shall be built again, and the wall, even in troublesome times. *Daniel 9:25* (Emphasis mine.)

History and the Bible record that four edicts were issued by the Persians to help restore and rebuild the Temple and Jerusalem.[28] The first edict was from Cyrus in 536 B.C., and focused on rebuilding the temple. Resistance in Israel was so severe that work had to be suspended.[29] Thus a second edict, also focused on restoring the Temple was issued by Darius in 519 B.C. This edict also failed. The next edict, by Artaxerxes in 457 B.C., sent Ezra to Jerusalem to appoint magistrates and reinstated the practice of Judaism. This was the act of religious significance to restore Jerusalem. For this and other reasons, the Adventists focused on the edict in 457 B.C.[30] They viewed the second edict of Artaxerxes in 444 or 445 B.C. (which was the fourth Persian edict) as merely broadening the work of reconstructing Jerusalem begun earlier.[31]

28. See *Ezra 1:1-4; 6:1-12; 7;* and *Nehemiah 2.*
29. *Ezra 4:19-24.*
30. C. A. Auberlen in *The Prophecies of Daniel and the Revelations of St. John.* (T. & T. Clark, 1856) contains a good review.
31. Others have used the date of the last edict as a starting point for this prophecy. The Biblical version of this edict is the most elaborate concerning the rebuilding of Jerusalem. Sir Robert Anderson (*The Coming Prince*, 14th ed., Kregel, 1954) dated Nehemiah's decree as Nisan 1 (March 14), 445 B.C., and moved ahead 173,3880 days (360 days x 69 weeks x 7 days) to April 6 32 A.D. which he cited as Christ's entry into Jerusalem. Others (e.g.

The prophecy in Daniel divides the seventy weeks into three parts: seven weeks, sixty two weeks (three-score and two), and one week. The Adventists found that, when using the formula of a day for a year, seven

---

Josh McDowell, *Evidence that Demands a Verdict*, Vol. 1 [Here's Life Publishers, 1979] pp. 170-175) dated the decree at Nisan 1 (March 5?) 444 B.C., and counted forward to Nisan 10 (March 30) 33 A.D., a probable date for the entry of Christ into Jerusalem and His crucifixion. The mathematics of this are complicated. McDowell's source took the 476 solar years difference between 444 B.C. and 33 A.D. (under common wisdom of losing a year in the process) and multiplied these by 365.242 to convert the years to days. He obtained 173,855 days, and then subtracted these from 173,880 to yield 25 days, which he added on to the end of March 5 to give a date which he says was the entry of Christ into Jerusalem. However: (1) These calculations assume that the edict, which some date at 444, is the correct beginning. While scholars disagree on the actual date of the decree, even more problematic is that the calculation *assumes* the date of the decree is the first of the Jewish month. (2) We also must account for the time of the prophecy in terms of elapsed days instead of years—a more natural assumption—and that these days are applied to the Jewish Calendar. Note that if the prophecy was not meant to be reckoned in terms of days, but in terms of solar years, if we begin at 444, it ends in 39/40 A.D., a year with no prophetic significance. (3) It is 69 weeks which marks the entry of Christ into Jerusalem. This collapses the ministry of Jesus into prophetic nonexistence; that is, with this interpretation Christ's ministry cannot be found in the prophecy, because Christ both enters and is crucified at 69 weeks (33 A.D.). The verses, however, say that Christ's ministry lasts one week (seven years). (4) This interpretation leaves entirely unanswered what to do with the seventieth week, thus providing the breeding ground for many fantastic theories. (5) Finally, this interpretation makes the mistake of severing the 70 weeks from the 2,300 days. If the 2,300 days are reckoned in the same way as suggested by McDowell, no prominent event is obtained.

weeks equalled forty-nine years, and that exactly forty-nine years after the 457 edict of Artaxerxes (i.e., in 408 B.C.) the streets of Jerusalem were restored. This restoration is recorded in the Book of Nehemiah, Chapter 13.

Continuing to build upon the numbers, they added sixty-two weeks (434 days) and with their formula arrived at the date 27 A.D., which they counted as the beginning of Christ's ministry. It is best to translate Hebrew to Gregorian (modern) years with a split year. Thus, a Hebrew religious year (from March-April to March-April) would fall between two Gregorian years, and the year above should be specified 26/27 A.D.[32] Seventy weeks brought them to the year 34 A.D. (Actually, the year 33/34 A.D.). In the year 34 A.D., they found the martyrdom of Stephen, considered by many as the formal rejection of the Gospel of Christ by the Sanhedrin. This, they thought, was a natural end for the prophecy.

Bahá'ís would make only a slight modification to the above. They hold that the seventy weeks ended with the crucifixion of Christ in 33 A.D., not the martyrdom of

32. Adventists used a slightly different reasoning to end with the year 27 A.D. Beginning at 457 B.C and going forward 483 years yields 26 A.D. (-457 + 483 = 26). But the Adventists argued that if the prophecy is built around full years, and 483 full years are required from 457 B.C., and if the prophecy begins at the first day of 457, it ends at the last day of 26 A.D. However, if it did not begin with the first day of 457, it will not end until 27 A.D. (See Smith, *The Prophecies of Daniel and the Revelation*, p. 219)

Stephen.[33] Bahá'ís begin the prophecy at 457 B.C., and move forward 490 years, ending at 33 A.D.[34] It is hard to date the martyrdom of Christ, but 33/34 A.D. is a date accepted by many.[35] The end of the sixty-nine weeks is not mentioned in the brief authoritative commentary Bahá'ís accept, but may date the beginning of John the Baptist's ministry, which is fixed by many at 27/28 A.D.[36]

Thus, from the time of the edict to rebuild Jerusalem, seventy weeks of years were marked for the people of Israel to make an end of sins. At that time they were offered everlasting righteousness if they responded to Jesus' ministry. They refused. The verses continue:

33. 'Abdu'l-Bahá writes (*Some Answered Questions*, p. 40): "To conclude, in the Book of Daniel from the rebuilding of Jerusalem to the martyrdom of Christ, seventy weeks are appointed; for by the martyrdom of Christ the sacrifice is accomplished and the altar destroyed." Later 'Abdu'l-Bahá writes (p. 41), ". . . the seventy weeks which came to an end with the ascension of Christ, when by His martyrdom the sacrifice and oblation ceased."

34. $457+33=490$.

35. *Scofield's Reference Bible* places the crucifixion at 29 A.D. James Price says the probable dates range from 27 to 33 A.D. (*Interpreting the New Testament* [Holt, Reinhart, and Winston, 1971].)

36. Luke (3:1) notes that, "in the fifteenth year of the reign of Tiberias Caesar . . . the word of God came to John." James Price notes, "Tiberius became emperor on August 19, A.D. 14. Luke therefore dates the beginning of John's mission in the year 28-29. Luke probably based his calculations on a synchronization of the Syrian and Roman calendars and intended the year 27-28." *Interpreting the New Testament*, p. 247.

> *And after threescore and two weeks shall Messiah be cut off*, but not for himself; and the people of the prince that shall come shall destroy the city and the sanctuary, and the end of it shall be with a flood, and unto the end of the war desolations are determined. And *he shall confirm the covenant with many for one week*; and in the midst of the week he shall cause the sacrifice and the oblation to cease, and for the overspreading of abominations he shall make it desolate, *even unto the consummation*, and that determined shall be poured upon the desolate. *Daniel 9:26-27* (Emphasis mine.)

These verses indicate that Christ will be cut off (i.e., killed) after sixty-two weeks. However, seven weeks already have been marked off from the beginning of the prophecy, so sixty-nine weeks have passed. This sixty-ninth week, we have seen, began in 27/28 A.D. We know little about the early ministry of Jesus, but we believe that the ministry of John the Baptist began in 27/28 A.D. If Christ's ministry began at about the same time, or if the ministry of John the Baptist may be subsumed as a part of the ministry of Christ, then Christ did confirm the covenant with many for one week (i.e., He taught for seven years). And in the midst of His work, Jesus was crucified. This occurred at the end of seventy weeks, in 33 A.D. Then, as the verses foretold, a prince came and destroyed Jerusalem. That prince was the Roman Titus.

A word more must be said about those who have used 444/445 B.C. as the beginning point of the prophecy of the seventy weeks. In order to arrive at dates that coincide with any actual historical events, they are forced to convert the years to days and apply them to the Jewish calendar. Using this method, they find that sixty-nine weeks coincides with the entry of Christ into Jerusalem. What then do we do with the seventieth week? Some very imaginative and fantastic suggestions have been put forth. Some require that the time period in the prophecy be interrupted until some time in the future, thus creating a gap in the last week which is at present almost two-thousand years old. There is no support for this in scripture. Some have further divided this last week in half, using the forty-two months (3.5 years) of Revelation as the dividing line. But there is another meaning for the forty-two months of Revelation (as we have discussed) and nowhere in Revelation does it speak of a lost week divided into two.

It is more important for us to consider the completion of the prophecy of the 2,300 days, of which the seventy weeks was but a part. While Jesus put an end to the daily sacrifice by His sacrifice, it is clear that the cleansing of the temple had not been completed. Thus, in the verses above Daniel announces that Israel will be punished until the *consummation* of these years. But when was that consummation? Adventists simply continued counting the 2,300 years—of which the 490 years (seventy weeks) was but a part—and arrived at the year 1844 A.D. They were right. But, they were disappointed.

When they could find no literal manifestation of the fulfillment of their prophecies in 1844, the Adventists lapsed into spiritual interpretations. They explained that judgment had arrived; that the heralding of the King of kings, foretold in the Book of Revelation (14:6-12), had occurred; and that the King of kings was at hand. But they could point to no obvious pronouncement of judgment, no real herald, and no living King of kings. Bahá'ís are in a better position. They can reveal all three.

A time-line chart of the fulfillment of this prophecy is presented in Table 8.1 which demonstrates how simple interpretation becomes once the starting points of the prophecies are known and simple solar years are used to mark the passage of the 2,300 days.

At the end of the Book of Daniel other sets of days are mentioned. Both 1,290 and 1,335 days are mentioned in a prophetic sense. Shortly, we will identify the meaning of these days.

Table 8.1

The Time Line Revealed in the Books of Daniel and Revelation

Artaxerxes order to rebuild Jerusalem	Reconstruction of Jerusalem Completed	Beginning of Ministry of Jesus	Crucifixion of Jesus		Herald of King of kings
457 B.C.	408 B.C.	27/28 A.D.	33/34 A.D.	622 A.D. 0 A.H.	1844 A.D. 1260 A.H.
Seven weeks (Dan 9:25)	After three score and two weeks shall Messiah be cut off . . . and unto the end of the war desolations are determined. (Dan 9:26)	And he shall confirm the covenant with many for one week; and in the midst of the week he shall cause sacrifice and oblation to cease . . . even until the consummation. (Dan 9:27)		And I will give power unto my two witnesses, and they shall prophesy a thousand two hundred and three score days (Rev 11:3)	
70 weeks (490 years) are dertermined upon thy people (Dan 9:24)					
Unto 2300 days (years): then shall the sanctuary be cleansed (Daniel 8:14)					

THE GREAT DAY OF WRATH
(*Revelation 6:1-17*)

Chapter 9

THE SECOND ADVENT

As the year 1844 approached, the Adventists awaited the return of Christ. But, another set of prophecies neared fulfillment in the East. For a thousand years Shí'í Muslims had waited for the return of the Twelfth Imam.

The eleventh Imam, Hasan al-'Askarí, known for his piety and nobility of character, had died a prisoner of the caliph in the city of Sakarra in the ninth century (260 A.H.).[1] By one account, the Imamate fell to his five-year-old son, Muḥammad. Refusing to believe that his father had died, the boy-Imam went looking for him in a cave from which he never returned. Shí'í prophecy claims that the Twelfth Imam will return at the end of time to vindicate the Shí'í claims and establish justice throughout the earth. He is known as the Mahdí (the guide), the Muntazzar (the Expected One), the Hujja (the Proof of Truth), and the Qá'im (the One who will arise). The year 1844 A.D. is the Muslim year 1260 A.H., exactly a thousand years after the disappear-

1. Ameer 'Alí, *The Spirit of Islam*, 1922, p. 346; Balyuzi, *Muḥammad and the Course of Islam*, 1976, p. 254.

ance of the Twelfth Imam. As the year approached, Muslim anticipation grew stronger.

The Qur'an itself fuels the speculation that the thousand-year period between 260 A.H. and 1260 A.H. is significant. Verses in the Qur'an indicate that for a thousand years the guidance of God given through the Imams will be absent. The verses read:

> God, He that created the heavens and the earth and what is between them in six days, then seated Himself upon the throne. Apart from Him you have no protector neither mediator; will you not remember? He directs the affair from heaven to earth, then it goes up to Him in one day, whose measure is *a thousand years* of your counting. *Qur'an 32:6* (Emphasis mine.)

The Dawn of The Third Day

It was a few hours before sunset on May 22, 1844 A.D. (1260 A.H.). Like the Magi of the Bible who approached Bethlehem looking for their Lord, a few devoted students, led by the prophecies of Islam, approached the Persian city of Shiraz. As they neared the city, one of the students, Mullá Ḥusayn, sent his companions ahead to find accommodations while he set off to take care of other matters. His companions left him. As Mullá Ḥusayn neared the city gate his eyes fell upon a radiant Youth who was about twenty-five years old. The Youth wore a green turban—the mark of a descendent of the Prophet Muḥammad.[2] He was, as the Bible had foretold, a "remnant of the seed" of Muḥammad.[3] He advanced toward Mullá Ḥusayn and embraced him. Mullá Ḥusayn thought that perhaps he was a fellow-student of his teacher who had been told of his approach. The Youth's name was Sayyid 'Alí-Muḥammad.[4]

Mullá Ḥusayn followed 'Alí-Muḥammad to His house. As they entered, the Youth quoted the Qur'an (15:46), "Enter therein in peace, secure." (The greeting that is given to Muslims when they enter paradise.) Mullá Ḥusayn told the youthful sayyid (descendant of the prophet Muḥammad) the story of his search for the promised Qá'im. He mentioned the signs by which he would know the Qá'im. It was about one hour after sunset. The Youth looked at Mullá Ḥusayn and

2. Islamic tradition about the Qá'im states, "The Apostle of God [Muḥammad], may God bless him and his family, said: The hour [of the end of the world] will not arise until the Mahdi from my descendants comes forth." (*The Kitáb al-Irshád*, London: The Muhammadi Trust of Great Britain and Northern Ireland, 1981, p. 543.)

3. "And the dragon was angry with the woman, and went to make war with the remnant of her seed, who keep the commandments of God, and have the testimony of Jesus Christ." *Revelation 12:17*

4. "The Prophet said, 'The world will not pass away until my community has been ruled by a man of my family whose name shall agree with mine.' " (John Alden Williams, *Themes of Islamic Civilization*, Berkeley: University of California Press, 1971, p. 205.)

declared with vibrant voice, "Behold, all these signs are manifest in Me!"

At first, the student did not understand. He was accustomed to doubt. No sooner had he voiced his doubts, however, than he found himself seized by fear and remorse, such as he could neither conceal nor explain. He vowed to alter his attitude and begged his Host to explain Himself. Sayyid 'Alí-Muḥammad slowly and patiently explained how all the signs of the Promised One were revealed in Him. Night gave way to morning as the Host chanted the verses of God with a voice that rose and fell in ethereal melodies. Mullá Ḥusayn was transformed; he forgot all thoughts of sleep and a profound sense of peace enveloped him.

At dawn 'Alí-Muḥammad turned to His disciple and revealed the titles by which both would be known, and the conditions for the beginning of His Ministry: "O thou who art the first to believe in Me! Verily I say, I am the Báb, the Gate of God, and thou art the Bábu'l-Báb, the gate of that Gate. Eighteen souls must, in the beginning, spontaneously and of their own accord, accept Me and recognize the truth of My Revelation. Unwarned and uninvited, each of these must seek independently to find Me. And when their number is complete, one of them must needs be chosen to accompany Me on My pilgrimage to Mecca and Medina. There I shall deliver the Message of God to the Sharíf of Mecca."[5] The Báb allowed Mullá Ḥusayn to depart,

5. Nabíl, *The Dawn-Breakers* (Wilmette, Ill.: Bahá'í Publishing Trust, 1939) p. 63.

but warned him not to divulge to any other soul that which he had seen or heard. Mullá Ḥusayn recorded his experience of this night:

> This Revelation, so suddenly and impetuously thrust upon me, came as a thunderbolt which, for a time, seemed to have benumbed my faculties. I was blinded by its dazzling splendour and overwhelmed by its crushing force. Excitement, joy, awe, and wonder stirred the depths of my soul. Predominant among these emotions was a sense of gladness and strength which seemed to have transfigured me. How feeble and impotent, how dejected and timid, I had felt previously! Then I could neither write nor talk, so tumultuous were my hands and feet. Now, however, the knowledge of His Revelation had galvanized my being. I felt possessed of such courage and power that were the world, all its peoples and its potentates, to rise against me, I would, alone and undaunted, withstand their onslaught. The universe seemed but a handful of dust in my grasp. I seemed to be the voice of Gabriel personified, calling unto all mankind: "Awake, for lo! the morning Light has broken. Arise, for His Cause is made manifest. The portal of His grace is open wide; enter therein O peoples of the world! For He who is your promised One is come!"[6]

6. Nabíl, *The Dawn-Breakers*, p. 65.

Prophecies From the East and West

This fateful meeting occurred on May 22, 1844, in the very year that the Edicts of Toleration were signed by the Sultan of Turkey. These edicts allowed the Jews to return to the Holy Land for the first time in nearly two-thousand years. Soon, millions of Jews would return to Israel.[7] The 2,300 years of desolation foretold by Daniel were ending. Israel was preparing to receive her Lord.

The desolation of Islam was ending too. While the domains of Islam had grown, the religion had been robbed of its spiritual heart at its very inception. While it had been successful in eliminating the idols we worshiped, it was unsuccessful in bringing the Kingdom of God to earth. Islam too was a temple whose outer court had been given over to Gentiles, while the work of its two prophet-witnesses, who alone could sanctify the temple, lay uncompleted. But this state of imperfec-

7. The Jewish historian Max Dimont writes, "The chain reaction from the idea of Zionism to the reality of Israel was touched off about 1860, at which time the messianic concept of a 'return to Zion' began to change into a political concept of a 'return to Palestine.' " The idea of returning to Palestine was not, however, a mere intellectual or political fancy. It was the Hand of God Himself that moved the Jews toward Israel. Great waves of immigration occurred. The first immigrants, in 1880-1900, were farmers. The second, 1900-1914, also were farmers. The third, 1918-1924, were city builders. The fourth, 1924-1939, were intellectuals and professionals. The last immigration dates from 1948 and continues still. (Dates from: *The Jews, God, and History*, New York: New American Library Inc., 1962, pp. 394-95.) These immigrations were made possible by the Edicts of Toleration.

tion would last but 1,260 years.[8] The two prophet-witnesses would return. The verses read:

> And after three days and a half the spirit of life from God entered into them [the two prophet witnesses], and they stood upon their feet, and great fear fell upon them who saw them. *Revelation 11:11*

The three and a half days are three and a half years which is forty-two months. Thus the prophecy deals again with the 1,260 days with which we are familiar. With the declaration of the Báb in 1260 A.H., we have the return of Muḥammad. With the Báb's foremost disciple, Quddús, we have the return of 'Alí. For 1,260 years, the special work of Islam, which was to give birth to the Redeemer, had been thwarted and the woman, who represents this work, had been forced to flee into the wilderness.[9] With the advent of the Báb, the Redeemer is delivered to us.

8. Recall Revelation 11:1-2: "And there was given me a reed like a rod; and the angel stood, saying, Rise, and measure the Temple of God, and the altar, and them that worship in it. But the court, which is outside the temple, leave out, and measure it not; for it is given unto the nations [Gentiles], and the holy city shall thy tread under foot forty and two months [1,260 days]." As we have seen, the 1,260 days are 1,260 years and the holy city is not the physical Jerusalem, but the promised heavenly Jerusalem which was the intended gift of Islam.

9. "And the woman fled into the wilderness, where she hath a place prepared by God, that they should feed her there a thousand two hundred and threescore days." *Revelation 12:6*

The Twofold Mission of the Báb

But if the Báb was the Messiah, what are the remaining symbols in Revelation? What about the third woe, the sounding of the seventh angel's trumpet, the last bowls of wrath, and the final battles between the Promised One, the beast, and the harlot—all of which the Book of Revelation has promised? The answer lies in the understanding that the Báb's ministry had a dual purpose.

As the Báb foretold, seventeen other disciples soon arose, and without direction or compulsion, advanced toward the sacred seat of Revelation. The Báb and His eighteen disciples are known collectively as the Letters of the Living.[10]

The Báb gathered His disciples together and sent them out into the world with these words:

> Ponder the words of Jesus addressed to His disciples, as He sent them forth to propagate the Cause of God. In such words as these, He bade them arise and fulfil their mission: "Ye are even as the fire which in the darkness of the night has been kindled upon the mountain top. Let your light shine before the eyes of men. Such must be the purity of your character and the degree of your renunciation, that the people of the earth may through you

10. Thus, there are nineteen Letters of the Living. The Báb counted Himself among them.

> recognize and be drawn closer to the heavenly Father who is the Source of purity and grace. For none has seen the Father who is in heaven. You who are His spiritual children must by your deeds exemplify His virtues, and witness to His glory. You are the salt of the earth, but if the salt has lost its savour, wherewith shall it be salted. Such must be the degree of your detachment, that into whatever city you enter to proclaim and teach the Cause of God, you should in no wise expect either meat or reward from its people. Nay, when you depart out of that city, you should shake the dust off your feet. As you have entered it pure and undefiled, so you must depart from that city." Nabíl, *The Dawn-Breakers*, pp. 92-93.

Thus, the instructions of the Báb to His disciples initially paralleled the instructions of Jesus to His. However, as the Báb continued, it became clear that His mission was different:

> O My Letters! Verily I say, immensely exalted is this Day above the days of the Apostles of old. Nay, immeasurable is the difference! You are the witnesses of the Dawn of the promised Day of God. You are the partakers of the mystic chalice of His Revelation. Gird up the loins of endeavour, and be mindful of the words of God, as revealed in His Book: "Lo,

> the Lord thy God is come, and with Him is the company of His angels arrayed before Him!" Purge your hearts of worldly desires and let angelic virtues be your adorning. Nabíl *The Dawn-Breakers*, p. 93.

The Day of which the Báb spoke was the same promised Day that Jesus foretold. The Báb, however, was proclaiming its arrival! The Kingdom had come, "on earth," not just in the heaven of the hearts of men.

The Báb told His disciples that they were the lowly of whom God had spoken in His Book, and that God would exalt them to great spiritual heights if they arose to trample every earthly desire, spoke not till God had spoken, and went forth to do God's bidding. Lastly, the Báb informed His disciples of His second mission:

> I am preparing you for the advent of a mighty Day. Exert your utmost endeavour that, in the world to come, I, who am now instructing you, may, before the mercy-seat of God, rejoice in your deeds and glory in your achievements. The secret of the Day is now concealed. It can neither be divulged nor estimated. The newly born babe of that Day excels the wisest and most venerable men of this time, and the lowliest and most unlearned of that period shall surpass in understanding the most erudite and accomplished of the divines of this age.

> Scatter throughout the length and breadth of this land, and, with steadfast feet and sanctified hearts, prepare the way for His coming. Heed not your weakness and frailty; fix your gaze upon the invincible power of the Lord, your God, the Almighty. Has He not, in past days, caused Abraham, in spite of His seeming helplessness, to triumph over the forces of Nimrod? Has He not enabled Moses, whose staff was his only companion, to vanquish Pharaoh and his hosts? Has he not established the ascendancy of Jesus, poor and lowly as He was in the eyes of men, over the combined forces of the Jewish people? Has he not subjugated the barbarous and militant tribes of Arabia to the holy and transforming discipline of Muḥammad, His Prophet? Arise in His name, put your trust wholly in Him, and be assured of ultimate victory." Nabíl, *The Dawn-Breakers*, p. 93-94.

Thus the Báb, the bringer of a mighty Day, was Himself the forerunner of another Day. The Sun of that Day lay just below the horizon, but the moment of its dawning was near. So it was to occur as scripture had foretold. In quranic terms, a second trumpet blast would follow closely upon the first.[11] In biblical terms,

11. "For the Trumpet shall be blown, and whosoever is in the heavens and whosoever is in the earth shall swoon, save whom

the third woe would follow fast upon the second.[12]

As foretold in the Bible, the Báb's ministry would be the later rain just before the harvest;[13] His would be the third day followed by the third night of Jonah;[14] He would be the third One to send forth servants to call people to the wedding feast prepared by God; the One Whose mission would immediately precede the arrival of the King.[15]

The Ministry of the Báb

The Báb's freedom was short-lived. Shortly after His return from proclaiming His mission in Mecca, He was arrested in His home city of Shiraz. Freed temporarily, he proceeded to Isfahan, where He was arrested again. Eventually, He was exiled and confined in a prison fortresses in the remote northwest of Persia. This did not

---

God wills. Then it shall be blown again, and lo, they shall stand beholding. And the earth shall shine with the Light of its Lord, and the Book shall be set in place, and the Prophets and witnesses shall be brought, and justly the issue be decided between them, and they not wronged." *Surah 39:67-70*

12. "The second woe is past and, behold, the third cometh quickly." *Revelation 11:14*

13. "Be patient therefore, brethren, unto the coming of the Lord. Behold, the husbandman waiteth for the precious fruit of the earth, and hath long patience for it, until he receive the early and latter rain. Be ye also patient; stablish your hearts: for the coming of the Lord draweth nigh." *James 5:6-7*

14. *Matthew 12:38ff.*

15. *Matthew 22:2ff.*

stop His flow of converts. People from far-off lands had visions of the Báb and began coming to Persia. Poets, enamored of stories of His ministry and teachings, began singing His praises. Great men and women were converted. The officials of the government and clergy, who were desirous of maintaining their positions, feared His influence. The prime minister of Persia worried that the shah himself might fall under the spell of the Báb.

The prime minister summoned the Báb to the city of Tabriz. There, before the heir to the throne and a selection of eminent clergy, the Báb was questioned. It was the same scene that Christ had faced two-thousand years before.

When the Báb entered the room, there was but one seat unfilled. This seat belonged to the heir to the throne, who had not yet arrived. The Báb, whom they intended to stand, advanced toward that seat and confidently sat down. The crowd fell into a deep, stunned silence as they contemplated the mysterious Being before them. Finally, someone asked Him, "Who do you claim to be, and what is the message you have brought?" The Báb replied:

> I am, I am, I am, the promised One! I am the One whose name you have for a thousand years invoked, at whose mention you have risen, whose advent you have longed to witness, and the hour of whose Revelation you have prayed God to hasten. Verily I say it is

> incumbent upon the peoples of both the East and the West to obey My word, and to pledge allegiance to My person. Nabíl, *The Dawn-Breakers*, pp. 315-316.

There could be no more question as to the claim of the Báb. A long silence ensued. Finally, the fated voice of arrogance was heard: "You wretched and immature lad of Shiraz! You have already convulsed and subverted Iraq; do you now wish to arouse a like turmoil in [this province]?" The Báb replied, "Your honour, I have not come hither of my own accord. I have been summoned to this place." The voice of arrogance spoke again: "Hold your peace you perverse and contemptible follower of Satan!" Then some of the clergy present decided to alter the tone of the proceedings. They asked the Báb to recite verses on the spot that would match in eloquence those of the Qur'an. This was a challenge which Muḥammad had made to those who claimed to be His equal. The Báb readily consented. He had gone no further than an introductory invocation when He was interrupted.

At this critical moment, judgment was passed on humankind. What did these learned scholars ask Him Who is the repository on earth of God's knowledge and the Herald of an Age of justice? They interrupted His recitation to argue with Him on a point of grammar! The scene became farcical. The Báb then recited these words from the Qur'an: "Far be the glory of thy Lord, the Lord of all greatness, from what they impute to

Him, and peace be upon His Apostles! And praise be to God, the Lord of the worlds." Then He rose and left the gathering.

The news of the Báb's public declaration to the assembly swept across the land. Back in Tabriz, the Báb was ordered beaten for His supposed insolence. The guards who had been present at the meeting refused to do this, so the chief mulla of the city of Tabriz did it himself. That very year, this same mulla became paralyzed and died in excruciating pain.

The Martyrdom of the Báb

Shortly after the Báb's public trial, the shah died and his prime minister was driven into exile. The new shah was seventeen years old and had been present at the interview of the Báb. His new prime minister, fearing the Báb's influence, decided to have Him killed. The Bible foretold the martyrdom of the Báb with these words about the return of the two prophet-witnesses after 1260 years (three and a half days):

> And they [the two prophet-witnesses who had returned] heard a great voice from heaven saying unto them, Come up here. And they ascended up to heaven in a cloud, and their enemies beheld them. And the same hour was there a great earthquake, and the tenth part of the city fell, and in the earthquake were

> slain of men seven thousand; and the remnant were terrified, and gave glory to God of heaven. The second woe is past and, behold, the third woe cometh quickly. *Revelation 11:12-14*

Both the Báb and Quddús suffered martyrdom in front of their enemies. In the symbolic language of prophecy, they were called to heaven in a cloud. Their enemies on earth were forced to behold that even their martyrdom could not destroy the cause of the Báb.

Recall now the prophecy in Revelation 1:7 that the Lord would come on clouds, and that even those that pierced Him would see Him.[16] Like Christ, the Báb came on the clouds of heaven. His true nature was veiled to many by the clouds of their imagination. Yet, His power was heavenly and His cause, like the movement of clouds, was majestic and unstoppable. Like Christ, as these verses reveal, the Báb's martyrdom was foreordained and His station was thereby glorified. Finally, we will see that those who pierced the Báb were unable to stop His cause. The religion of the Báb grew rapidly even after His death and, through the Bahá'í Faith, continues still to grow.

As the Báb was led to the barracks which was to be the scene of His martyrdom, a youth named Anís approached Him, pleading, "Send me not from Thee, O

16. "Behold, he cometh with clouds; and every eye shall see him, and they also which pierced him; and all kindreds of the earth shall wail because of him. Even so, Amen."

Master. Wherever Thou goest, suffer me to follow Thee." The Báb granted this wish and replied: "Arise, and rest assured that you will be with Me. Tomorrow you shall witness what God has decreed." Four companions of the Báb were placed with Him in a cell in the barracks. The Báb ordered one of them not to confess his faith, in order that we may have an account of what happened. This man, Sayyíd Ḥusayn, related the following:

> That night the face of the Báb was aglow with joy, a joy such as never shone from His countenance. Indifferent to the storm that raged about Him, He conversed with us with gaiety and cheerfulness. The sorrows that had weighed so heavily upon Him seemed to have completely vanished. Their weight appeared to have dissolved in the consciousness of the approaching victory.[17]

On the morning of the martyrdom, the Báb was engaged in confidential conversation with Sayyid Ḥusayn when a soldier came to take Him away. The Báb said to the soldier, "Not until I have said to him [Sayyid Ḥusayn] all those things that I wish to say can any earthly power silence Me. Though all the world be armed against Me, yet shall they be powerless to deter Me from fulfilling, to the last word, My intention."[18] The soldier was amazed, but removed Sayyid Ḥusayn

17. Nabíl, *The Dawn-Breakers*, p. 508.
18. Nabíl, *The Dawn-Breakers*, p. 509.

from the presence of the Báb. The Báb was brought to the civil and ecclesiastical chiefs of Tabriz. They cowered in His presence and refused to confront Him directly on that fateful day.

The Báb spoke with His intended executioner, who had come to know of Him and was curious to meet Him. The man approached the Báb and said, "I profess the Christian Faith, and entertain no ill will against you. If your Cause be the Cause of Truth, enable me to free myself from the obligation to shed your blood."[19] The Báb replied: "Follow your instructions, and if your intention be sincere, the Almighty is surely able to relieve you from your perplexity."

A nail was pounded into a wall of the barracks and the Báb and His companion, Anís, were suspended from it. Seven hundred and fifty gunmen lined up in three rows. As more than ten-thousand people watched, peering over the walls of the courtyard and from the rooftops of houses, the command to fire was given. The noonday sun was hidden by the smoke of the rifles. When the smoke cleared, the companion of the Báb stood uninjured upon the ground, and the Báb Himself had vanished.

The soldiers searched frantically, and finally found the Báb back in His own cell. He was talking with Sayyid Ḥusayn. Looking up at His captors, He said, "I have finished My conversation with Sayyid Ḥusayn. Now you may proceed to fulfill your intention."

The people were convinced they had witnessed a

19. Nabíl, *The Dawn-Breakers*, p. 512.

miracle. A colonel decided to still the crowd by producing the Báb and drawing up a different regiment to complete the execution. The Báb again was suspended with His companion, and seven hundred and fifty gunmen were produced. The Báb addressed the crowd: "Had you believed in Me, O wayward generation, every one of you would have followed the example of this youth, who stood in rank above most of you, and willingly would have sacrificed himself in My path. The day will come when you will have recognized Me; that day I shall have ceased to be with you." The soldiers fired. The two bodies were mingled together by the bullets; only their faces remained untouched. A fierce gale swept across the city.

It is said that an earthquake occurred at the death of Jesus.[20] History does not record such a physical earthquake. The earthquake was spiritual. The Book of Revelation also promises us an end-time earthquake: A tenth of the city, seven-thousand people are to be slain.[21] This too is primarily a spiritual matter and has many meanings. But in Bahá'í writings, earthquakes tend to symbolize the crisis in faith that attends the transition from one spiritual leader to another.[22] The

20. *Matthew 27:51.*

21. *Revelation 11:13*, quoted above.

22. For example, in interpreting another passage in Revelation (11:19) where there is a transition in the leaders of the faith, 'Abdu'l-Bahá writes, "the earthquake of doubts will take place, a hail of torments will beat upon the violators of the Covenant, and even those who profess belief will fall into trials and temptations." *Some Answered Questions*, p. 61.

slain then, may refer to those who abandoned their faith at the martyrdom of the Báb. The rest, we are told, "gave glory to the God of heaven." There is, as we shall see, great meaning in these words. There was, however, a literal fulfillment to this prophecy. A few years later, in the city which first rejected and persecuted the Báb, there was a mighty earthquake which killed many thousands.

Soon after the martyrdom of the Báb, hundreds of His followers were executed. In the first twenty years of the Faith which the Báb authored, twenty-thousand followers would be put to death solely on account of their allegiance to Him and His Cause.

When the Báb was martyred, He had just begun His seventh year of ministry. An Islamic tradition foretold that the rule of the Qá'im would last for seven years.[23]

Was the Báb the Returned Christ?

Any fair observer will find it difficult to ignore the parallels between the Ministry of the Báb and that of Christ. Each man preached a gospel of salvation based

23. "I asked Abú 'Abd Alláh (Jafar al-Sádiq), peace be upon him: 'How long will the one who will arise (*qá'im*), peace be upon him, rule?' 'Seven years,' he answered, 'but the days will lengthen for him so that one of his years will be the same length as ten of your years'" *The Kitáb al-Irshád*, p. 550. The first part of the hadith is accurate. The lengthening occurred through the Ministry of Bahá'u'lláh, but the ten to one formula appears to be wrong.

upon belief in Him and action upon His word. Each touched the hearts and transformed the souls of all who sought Him. Each gathered disciples who were transformed into heroes of God, who went forth to proclaim the Kingdom of God to those who would ultimately kill them. Each spoke with certainty about the nearness of the Kingdom of God. Each performed miraculous works and stood alone against an onslaught of enemies. Each drew around Him thousands of followers. The life of each was cut short by the machinations of those who feared His power and misunderstood His Cause. Each was publicly executed. As the followers of each gathered together after the execution of their Leader, they found that their Deliverer walked still within their hearts. Thousands of the followers of each were subsequently put to death, but causes of each continued to grow in the face of relentless persecution. And finally, once again, the enemies of each were leaders of church and state. But this last time they were not Romans and Jews; they were Muslims.

It is obvious therefore that we must consider the Báb as the returned Christ. Bahá'í writings support this claim.[24] As we have before explained, the Book of

24. The authorized interpreter of the Bahá'í Faith, 'Abdu'l-Bahá writes: "You have written that there is a difference among the believers concerning the "Second Coming of Christ." Gracious God! Time and again this question hath arisen, and its answer hath emanated in a clear and irrefutable statement from the pen of 'Abdu'l-Bahá, that what is meant by the 'Lord of Hosts' and the 'Promised Christ' is the Blessed Perfection (Bahá'u'lláh) and His holiness the Exalted One (the Báb)." *The World Order of Bahá'u'lláh*, Wilmette, Il.: Bahá'í Publishing Trust, 1974, p. 139.

Revelation (12:5) referred to the child born from the woman who fled into the wilderness for 1,260 days/years as "the male child who was to rule all nations with a rod of iron." In Christian thought, this male child is the Christ returned. This child was the Báb.

Two End-Time Events

As stunning as it is to realize that the Báb is the Return of Christ, there is more to come. If we look closely at scripture, we find there is an event of even greater significance: the incomprehensible appearance of the Father. It is two events, not one, that we are promised at the end times.

Consider first the words to Titus (2:13): "Looking for that blessed hope, and that glorious appearing of the great God *and* our savior Jesus Christ." (Emphasis mine.) Does this verse refer to one event or two? If we suspend the force of tradition, which has taught us to expect only one event, we see that the verse could be speaking of two events: the return of Christ and the appearance of the Father.

Consider also these verses in First Corinthians:

> For as in Adam all die, even so in Christ shall all be made alive; But every man in his own order: Christ the first fruits; afterward they that are Christ's at his coming. Then cometh

> the end, when he shall have delivered up the kingdom to God, even the Father, when he shall have put down all authority and power. *I Corinthians 15:22-24*

Note the order of occurrences: First the early Christians would suffer—the first fruits of the Christ's Ministry—then Christ would return; then the Father would appear to rule the nations, and the returned Christ would yield up His Kingdom to the Father. Again, the prophecy indicates two events: the return of Christ and the appearance of the Father who comes to reign.

Consider also the testimony in Timothy which indicates that the function of the returned Christ would be to show the way, during His Ministry, to the King of Kings, who would come after Him. The verses read:

> Thou that keep this commandment without spot, unrebukeable, until the appearance of our Lord Jesus Christ; Which *in his times* he shall show who is the blessed and only Potentate, the King of kings and Lord of lords. *I Timothy 6:14-15*

Recall, also, that in the Book of Revelation the third and final woe, which is the coming of the Father, falls shortly after the second.[25] The first woe was the Reve-

25. *Revelation 11:14*: "The second woe is past and behold, the third woe cometh quickly."

lation of Muḥammad. The second was the Revelation of the Báb. Soon we will identify the third Revelation, which occurred just a few years after the Revelation of the Báb.

When we in the West speak of the return of Christ, it is actually to the latter of these two events that we refer. It is the return of Christ *in the Glory of the Father*. Scripture, however, clearly reveals that the appearance of the Father would come *after* the return of Christ. The Báb was that first return.

Chapter 10

THE HIDDEN MYSTERY

Recall for a moment the last trumpet blasts of the Book of Revelation. The sounding of the sixth's angel's trumpet brings retribution against humanity because we still have not repented of our misdeeds. This trumpet blast refers to the Revelation of the Báb. But then the scripture shows us a wondrous thing. Another angel appears who possesses many of the attributes of God Himself.[1] The verses read:

> And I saw another mighty angel come down from heaven clothed with a cloud; and a rainbow was upon his head, and his face was as though it were the sun, and his feet like pillars of fire. And he had in his hand a little scroll open; and he set his right foot upon the sea, and his left foot on the earth, And cried out with a loud voice, as when a lion roareth; and when he had cried, seven thunders had uttered their voices. And when the seven thunders had uttered their voices, I was about to write;

1. Notes on the similarity of the characteristics of this Angel to God are found in Chapter 3.

> and I heard a voice from heaven saying unto me, *Seal up those things which the seven thunders uttered,* and write them not. *Revelation 10:1-4* (Emphasis mine.)

We know that this mighty Angel is not God because later He swears by God. Who is He? Why does He appear during the ministry of the Báb? Why does He appear in such godly attire? And why cannot the mystery of what He says be revealed?

The Báb's first act was to send His first disciple to the city of Tehran to proclaim the new Message and to present to the holiest soul he could find a special tablet. The Báb told His disciple that in Tehran he would find, "a Mystery of such transcendent holiness as neither Hijaz [the place of Muḥammad's Revelation] or Shiraz [the place of the Báb's Revelation] can hope to rival."[2] Through discussion with the residents of Tehran, the disciple soon learned of One Whose character shone through the darkness of the times, and the Holy Soul was found. His name was Mírzá Ḥusayn-'Alí, and today He is known by the title "Bahá'u'lláh," which means "the Glory of God."[3]

Bahá'u'lláh was a son of the minister of state. Upon His father's death, the ministry had been offered to Bahá'u'lláh, but He refused it. He was not interested

2. Nabíl, *The Dawn-Breakers*, p. 96.

3. Mírzá Ḥusayn-'Alí gave Himself this title at the conference of Badas͟ht. The title was confirmed by the Báb.

in the intrigues of the state.[4] His nature guided Him to more important tasks. He spent His time cheering the disconsolate, feeding the hungry, and befriending the stranger. He later would counsel His followers, "*Tell the rich of the midnight sighing of the poor, lest heedlessness lead them into the path of destruction.*"[5]

When Bahá'u'lláh was given the Tablets of the Báb, He did not need to study them: He intuitively knew the Source and immediately proclaimed them to be from God and arose to spread the divine teachings abroad. How different was His response from that of the masses who heard the Báb's summons and failed to act.

Two Suns in the Sky

For awhile during the ministry of the Báb, there were two Suns in the sky, giving the same light. Both the Báb and Bahá'u'lláh shed light upon all humankind. The personality of Bahá'u'lláh perhaps is best known by the effect He had upon people. His enchanting radiance and the ease of His understanding of the Revelation of the Báb are legendary. The head mujtahid (doctor of Islamic law) of Bahá'u'lláh's province was warned that "whoever attains his presence falls immediately under his spell."[6] The mujtahid, fearing the destruction of

4. See the testimony of Bahá'u'lláh's activities in *The Dawn-Breakers*, pp. 86-108.

5. Bahá'u'lláh, *The Hidden Words*, Persian #49 (Wilmette, Il.: Bahá'í Publishing Trust, 1954).

6. Nabíl, *The Dawn-Breakers*, p. 113.

Islam, sent two of his favored disciples to gather information. As they approached the home of Bahá'u'lláh, they found Him revealing a commentary on a verse in the Qur'an. The two disciples sat, listened, and were transformed by His words. They vowed then and there to dedicate their lives to Bahá'u'lláh and never returned to their former master. Many others followed suit.

As Bahá'u'lláh neared Karbila one day on a teaching trip, a young convert spoke to his Muslim father about Bahá'u'lláh's visit saying, "O my father, there is an honourable person from Tehran, although wearing a kulah, not a turban [a turban is the headgear of a mulla], is a surging sea of divine knowledge; he has a shining countenance, and a radiance of joy and happiness is with him, surely we should go to see him." His father, who was a very devout Muslim, only assented reluctantly. Yet upon entering the presence of Bahá'u'lláh, he was transformed. He knew Whom he had found, and immediately he forgot his fanatical beliefs and went forth to proclaim his new Faith. When his son later was martyred for his religion, the father gave thanks to God that his sacrifice had been accepted at the divine threshold.[7]

Another time Bahá'u'lláh came upon a dervish who was eating. That dervish became so enamored of Bahá'u'lláh that he forsook his cooking utensils and straight away arose to follow his Lord.[8] This is uncom-

7. Lady Blomfield, *The Chosen Highway* (Wilmette, Il.: Bahá'í Publishing Trust, 1970) pp. 196-197.

8. Blomfield, *The Chosen Highway*, p. 118.

mon love. Each day more and more people became intoxicated with the joyous wine of Bahá'u'lláh's presence, and thus each day more and more people drew closer to discovering the Mystery of Tehran.

Who was this mystery of God in Tehran? He was the Promised Angel of Revelation 10, come down from heaven clothed with a cloud: which means that His identity was veiled. And though He cried out with a loud voice proclaiming the advent of the Promised Day, yet (as scripture had foretold) the identity of this Angel of God could not yet be made known. The time to reveal His Reality had not yet come. The Bible records that this mighty Angel, who arose during the ministry of the Báb, could not be revealed until the time had come for the sounding of the seventh angel. The verses read:

> And the angel whom I saw standing upon the sea and upon the earth lifted up his hand to heaven. And swore by him that liveth forever and ever, who created heaven and the things that are in it, and the earth and the things that are in it, and the sea and the things that are in it, that there should be delay no longer; *But in the days of the voice of the seventh angel, when he shall begin to sound, the mystery of God should be finished*, as he hath declared to his servants the prophets. *Revelation 10:5-7* (Emphasis mine.)

As the time of the seventh angel neared, however, some people began to guess the identity of Bahá'u'lláh. The Báb had promised an old man that he would meet the promised Ḥusayn, the one who was to come after the Qá'im. It was a year after the martyrdom of the Báb, in the city of Karbila, when this promise was fulfilled. The old man, Shaykh Ḥasan, grants us this priceless description of Bahá'u'lláh:

> While I was passing by the gate of the inner courtyard of the shrine of the Imam Ḥusayn [the grandson of Muḥammad], my eyes, for the first time, fell upon Bahá'u'lláh. What shall I recount regarding the countenance I beheld! The beauty of that face, those exquisite features which no pen or brush dare describe, His penetrating glance, His kindly face, the majesty of His bearing, the sweetness of His smile, the luxuriance of His jet-black flowing locks, left an indelible impression upon my soul. I was then an old man, bowed with age. How lovingly He advanced towards me! He took me by the hand and, in a tone which at once betrayed power and beauty, addressed me in these words: "This very day I have purposed to make you known as a Bábí throughout Karbila." Still holding my hand in His, He continued to converse with me. He walked with me all along the market street, and in the end He said: "Praised be to God that you have remained in Karbila, and have beheld with your own eyes the countenance of the promised Ḥusayn."[9]

9. Nabíl, *The Dawn-Breakers*, pp. 32-33.

To those who had recognized Him, Bahá'u'lláh replied: "Not yet." Not until the time of the seventh angel could the secret of Bahá'u'lláh's identity be made manifest. The man who recognized the station of Bahá'u'lláh continues his account:

> These words of Bahá'u'lláh moved me to the depths of my being. I felt impelled to proclaim to a heedless people, at that very moment and with all my soul and power, the advent of the promised Ḥusayn. He bade me, however, repress my feelings and conceal my emotions. "Not yet," He breathed into my ears; "the appointed hour is approaching. It has not yet struck. Rest assured and be patient." From that moment all my sorrows vanished. My soul was flooded with joy. In those days I was so poor that most of the time I hungered for food. I felt so rich however, that all the treasures of the earth melted away into nothingness when compared with that which I already possessed.[10]

There is a prayer that many Bahá'ís recite daily, the Long Obligatory Prayer. Part of it reads:

> I testify unto that whereunto have testified all created things, and the Concourse on high, and the inmates of the all-highest Paradise, and beyond them the Tongue of Grandeur itself from the all-glorious Horizon, that

10. Nabíl, *The Dawn-Breakers*, p.

> Thou art God, that there is no God but Thee, and *that He Who hath been manifested is the Hidden Mystery*, the Treasured Symbol, through Whom the letters B and E (Be) hath been joined and knit together. I testify that it is He Whose name hath been set down by the Pen of the Most High, and *Who hath been mentioned in the Books of God*, the Lord of the Throne on high and of earth below. (Emphasis mine.)

I believe that the Hidden Mystery is the same mystery of God the Bible spoke of so long ago. In the early days of the Bábí Faith, the identity of Bahá'u'lláh was that Mystery. The Mystery is now disclosed.

The Seventh Angel Sounds

The time between the two Manifestations of God had been unalterably fixed by the Hand of God. In one of His tablets, addressed "To Him Who Will Be Made Manifest," the Báb explicitly stated the duration of this time. In this tablet the Báb asked God: "Though no doubt is there about it," let there be "granted a respite of nineteen years as a token of Thy favor" between the Revelations.[11]

11. The Báb, *Selections from the Writings of the Báb* (Haifa: Bahá'í World Center, 1976) pp. 6-8.

There would be nineteen years separating the first great Revelation, beginning in 1844, and the second which would begin in 1863. This very span of time had been predicted in Islamic tradition as the length of time of the rule of the Qá'im.[12] The third woe of the Book of Revelation would indeed follow quickly upon the second.

Jesus did not proclaim His station immediately after His baptism by John, when He was anointed. Time elapsed before Christ's proclamation could be made publicly. Jesus wandered forty days and forty nights after His baptism before He began His Ministry. And even when He began preaching, it was only near the end of His Ministry that public proclamations of his true station were made. There was a moment of testing when Jesus asked Peter who he thought Jesus was. Similarly, it was only at the end of the Ministry of the Báb that He made a public declaration.

Bahá'u'lláh was anointed by God in the infamous Black Pit of Tehran, a subterranean, foul dungeon where the empire's worst criminals were kept.[13] A full ten years elapsed between His anointment in the Black Pit and His declaration to His followers in 1863. This, too, was part of prophecy. The year 1863/1864 of the

12. A Muslim book of prophecy, the Kitáb al-Irshád, states, "It is reported that the period of time of the state of the Qá'im will be nineteen years, whose days will be lengthened as we have already described." (p. 554) The days were lengthened by Bahá'u'lláh.

13. This pit was known as the Síyáh-Chál.

Christian calendar is the year 1280 of the Muslim calendar and falls 1,290 years after the proclamation of Muḥammad.[14] Thus 1,290 years passed from the proclamation of the mission of Muḥammad to the proclamation of the mission of Bahá'u'lláh. The Book of Daniel had indicated that it would be so:

> And from the time that the daily sacrifice shall be taken away, and the abomination that maketh desolate be set up, there shall be a thousand two hundred and ninety days.
> *Daniel 12:11*

The proclamation of Muḥammad took away the daily sacrifice. It marked the end of a prophetic trust that had resided with the Jews from Abraham to Jesus. Through the dispensation of Islam, Israel lay desolate as a consequence of Jewish misdeeds which extended all the way back to the time of Jesus. However, this desolation was to have an end. Israel was again to receive the favor of God and the ancient promises to Israel would be fulfilled.

Lest we think that it was Israel only that was made desolate, let us remind ourselves that the domains of Islam have fared little better. The whole area is awaiting regeneration. Before this can happen, Jews and

14. The ministry of Muḥammad began ten years before His flight to Medina, which began the Islamic calendar.

Muslims, whose ancestors were brothers, must come to believe again in a common destiny. It was Abraham that began their common journey together; it is Bahá'u'lláh who has come to complete it. If the two groups will not reconcile, horrors of apocalyptic dimension are in store for us all.

By Way of the Gate

Let us now review the biblical perspective of what has happened in the twin appearances of the Báb and Bahá'u'lláh. It has happened as Ezekiel foretold, that the Glory of God (Bahá'u'lláh) came by the way of the Gate (the Báb) from the East (Persia is east of Israel). The verses read:

> Afterward, he brought me to the gate, even the gate that looketh toward the east. And behold, the Glory of the God of Israel came from the way of the east; and his voice was like a noise of many waters, and the earth shined with His glory. *Ezekiel 43:1-2*

It is Bahá'u'lláh who is the Central Figure of the Bahá'í Faith. He is, Bahá'ís believe, the object of the host of biblical prophecies concerning the Promised One returned in the Glory of the Father. And now the persistent dating of the new age with the sixth event in

Revelation begins to make sense. For not only did the Báb inaugurate the era of Bahá'u'lláh, the two ministries may be seen as continuations of one Revelation.[15] Lastly, we note that the entire Bahá'í world follows a calendar which begins its reckoning at the appearance of the Báb.

15. There are many places in the Bahá'í writings where this thought is expressed. For example, the Báb Himself, in a mystical identification, wrote: "He [Bahá'u'lláh] is I and I am He." While this is true, the Báb, in the same tablet, makes plain that when viewed in another light: "I Myself am, verily, but a ring upon the hand of Him Whom God shall make manifest [a title of Bahá'u'lláh]—glorified be His mention." *Selections from the Writings of the Báb*, p. 168.

Chapter 11

THE THIRD ADVENT

When Bahá'u'lláh announced that He was the Promised One, it was during a twelve-day period in April of 1863. The scene was an island in the river Tigris in the city of Baghdad. Only His close followers were present. The world was still unaware of what had happened. That silence soon would end.

When Bahá'u'lláh proclaimed His identity, He was on His way into exile. The sultan of Turkey, under influence from Persian officials, feared that Bahá'u'lláh's presence near Persia would cause the religion of the Báb to reignite. When Bahá'u'lláh made His proclamation, He already had been summoned to Constantinople (Istanbul), the capital of the Turkish Empire. Once there, He was exiled to Adrianople (Edirne) in Europe. Finally, He was exiled to the worst prison in the Turkish Empire: a prison city called 'Akká in Palestine. It was from Adrianople, and later from 'Akká, that Bahá'u'lláh wrote to the kings and rulers of the world.

These proclamations were bold. Bahá'u'lláh states: "Never since the beginning of the world hath the Message been so openly proclaimed."[1] These tablets were a direct call to the leading sovereigns of the world, who because of their claims to be Christian or Muslim, should have been expecting the call from their Lord. So powerful and transforming were these tablets that Bahá'u'lláh designated each with a special name.[2]

> The first hath been named "The Rumbling," the second "the Blow," the third "the Inevitable," the fourth "the Plain," the fifth "the Catastrophe," and the others "The Stunning Trumpet-Blast," "The Near Event," "The Great Terror," "The Trumpet," "The Bugle," and the like so that all the peoples of the earth may know, of a certainty, and may witness, with outward and inner eyes, that He Who is the Lord of Names hath prevailed, and will continue to prevail, under all conditions, over all men.[3]

In the biblical parable of the wedding feast, a king sends out messengers to ask those who were bidden to the feast to attend.[4] A king, it is natural to assume, would invite other kings to the wedding feast of his son. In a similar manner, Bahá'u'lláh began His Ministry by inviting the kings of the earth to the banquet prepared by God, so that through these kings the peoples of the

1. Shoghi Effendi, *God Passes By* (Wilmette, Il.: Bahá'í Publishing Trust, 1944) p. 212.
2. Shoghi Effendi, *The Promised Day is Come* (Wilmette, Il.: Bahá'í Publishing Trust, 1980) p. 46.
3. Shoghi Effendi, *The Promised Day Is Come*, p. 46.
4. See *Matthew 22:2-14* and *Luke 14:15-24*.

earth would find peace. The prophecy foretold the results. Those who were bidden did not come.

As we noted earlier, kings and rulers are the earthly stars to whom most of humankind looks for guidance. From His places of confinement Bahá'u'lláh wrote the kings and rulers of the world, including the rulers who had banished Him: Nasíru'd-Dín, the Shah of Iran, and 'Abdu'l-Azíz, the Sultan of Turkey. He summoned each of these leaders to the Cause of God and warned them of their downfall if they did not respond with justice to the Call of God.

To date, only one king and one queen have entered the shelter prepared by the Glory of God: Malietoa Tanumafili III of Western Samoa and Queen Marie of Rumania. The Queen wrote:

> If ever the name of Bahá'u'lláh or 'Abdu'l-Bahá comes to your attention, do not put their writings from you. Search out their books, and let their glorious, peace-bringing, love-creating words and lessons sink into your hearts as they have into mine . . . Seek them and be the happier.[5]

It is not my purpose to review in detail the many tablets which Bahá'u'lláh wrote to the kings and rulers of the world. Masterly and authoritative books are available which review these tablets in far greater detail than space allows here.[6] In this section, I wish to communi-

5. In Shoghi Effendi, *God Passes By*, p. 391.

6. See *The Proclamation of Bahá'u'lláh* (Haifa: Bahá'í World Center, 1972) and Shoghi Effendi, *The Promised Day Is Come.*

cate only a token of the majesty, beauty, compelling power, and urgency in these magnificent tablets. Furthermore, as Bahá'ís have an authoritative commentary on these tablets, I have tried to preserve some of the wording from this commentary in my short sketch.

The Star Fall

Each tablet to a ruler generally begins with a summons and a proclamation of the station of Bahá'u'lláh. In some, Bahá'u'lláh presents Himself as a perfect Servant of the Almighty, doing His bidding. For example, to the Sultan of Turkey (who was Bahá'u'lláh's captor), He wrote: "Hearken O king, to the speech of Him that speakest the truth, Him that doth not ask thee to recompense Him with the things God hath chosen to bestow upon thee, Him Who unerringly treadeth the straight Path."

To other rulers, the summons may begin more directly as a call from God Himself. The introduction of the tablet to the ruler of Russia reads: "O Czar of Russia! Incline thine ear unto the voice of God, the King, the Holy, and turn thou unto Paradise, the Spot wherein He Who, among the Concourse on high, beareth the most excellent titles, and Who, in the kingdom of creation, is called by the name of God, the Effulgent, the All-Glorious." (Note that at no time does Bahá'u'lláh claim to be God. His statements amply demonstrate that God is immeasurably exalted above His Chosen

Ones.[7] However, God's Chosen Ones can and do speak with the Voice of God. Indeed, the Voice of God's Chosen One is all we will ever know of the Voice of God.)

Following the summons there appears in each tablet a set of hopes, admonitions, and prescriptions for the sovereign and his or her people. The counsels are sometimes general, sometimes specific. The kings are told to embrace the new Cause, to arise and champion it, and to aid the followers of Bahá'u'lláh in every land. They are told that the solutions to their problems can be found only in the teachings of this new Faith. And sometimes they are told the broad outline of what God desires them to do. For example, they are asked to abandon riches, to seek counsel only from God-fearing people, not to aggrandize their ministers at the expense of their subjects, to establish justice, to take care of the poor, to reduce their armaments, and to act in a manner that is befitting their station as God's shadow on earth.

Finally, many of the tablets contain specific pro-

7. Bahá'u'lláh writes, "Ten thousand Prophets, each a Moses, are thunderstruck upon the Sinai of their search at His [God's] forbidding voice, 'Thou shalt never behold Me!'; whilst a myriad Messengers, each as great as Jesus, stand dismayed upon their heavenly thrones by the interdiction, 'Mine Essence thou shalt never apprehend!' From time immemorial He hath ever been veiled in the ineffable sanctuary of His exalted Self, and will everlastingly continue to be wrapt in the impenetrable mystery of His inaccessible Reality." *Gleanings from the Writings of Bahá'u'lláh*, pp. 62-63.

phetic warnings and judgments against the sovereign and those who will follow him or her. I will cite but a few of many examples. We would do well to consider what happened to the Shah of Iran. The shah's reign had begun with the execution of the Báb and the imprisonment of Bahá'u'lláh in a pit in the center of Tehran reserved for the worst prisoners. It continued with the banishment of Bahá'u'lláh from Iran. The shah's rule spelled death for more than twenty-thousand followers of the infant Faith of the Báb and Bahá'u'lláh. The shah responded to the tablet of Bahá'u'lláh by having the Bahá'í messenger who delivered it killed. The messenger's name was Badí. A photograph exists of his luminous face as he was under torture before he was killed. As Bahá'u'lláh testified, God soon would make of the shah "an object-lesson for the world." On the eve of a celebration, the shah intended to be one of the greatest in the history of Persia, he was assassinated. His dead body was propped in his carriage and driven back to his palace. The political revolution that followed brought the end of the 130-year reign of the Qájár dynasty.[8]

The next to persecute Bahá'u'lláh was the Sultan of Turkey, 'Abdu'l-Aziz. The tablet addressed to him

8. The shah's assassination did not happen immediately after receipt of the tablet. An earlier misdeed of three Bábís, who made a farcical attempt to assassinate the shah, had given him reason to act against Bábís and Bahá'ís. Bahá'u'lláh wrote that the misdeed of the three Bábís forestalled judgment against the shah. (See Shoghi Effendi, *The Promised Day is Come*, pp. 60-70.)

foretold the catastrophe soon to befall him and his country. The tablet reads:

> The day is fast approaching when the Land of Mystery [Adrianople] and what is beside it shall be changed and shall pass out of the lands of the king, and commotion shall appear, and the voice of lamentation shall be raised, and the evidences of mischief shall be revealed on all sides, and confusion shall spread by reason of that which hath befallen these captives [the Bahá'ís] at the hands of the hosts of oppression. The course of things shall be altered, and conditions wax so grievous, that the very sands on the desolate hills will moan, and the trees on the mountain will weep, and blood will flow out of all things. Then wilt thou behold the people in sore distress.
>
> Soon, will He seize you in His wrathful anger, and sedition will be stirred up in your midst, and your dominions will be disrupted . . . Erelong will ye behold that which hath been sent down from the Pen of My command. Bahá'u'lláh, in *The Promised Day Is Come*, p. 61.

The ink of the tablet had barely dried before an internal revolution led to the assassination of the monarch and the rapid dissolution of the once mighty Ottoman Empire. Its territories were dismembered, its sultans dethroned, and both the caliphate and the sultanate (a rulership that had remained unbroken for six and a half centuries) were extinguished.[9] The Land of Mystery (Adrianople), mentioned by Bahá'u'lláh in the tablet, soon was occupied by Russian troops. Serbia, Montenegro, and Romania proclaimed their independence. Bulgaria became self-governing and later achieved independence. Cyprus and Egypt were occupied. The French took over Tunis. Bosnia and Herzegovina were lost to Austria. Blood spilled profusely, and the empire which had been propped up by a series of degenerate successors fell into ever-increasing ruin as the judgment of God continued against it.

It is said that when Napoleon III, the most powerful sovereign of the time, received his first tablet from Bahá'u'lláh, he threw it behind his back and said, "If this is from God, I am two Gods." An answer to his insolence is found in a second tablet to the emperor. Bahá'u'lláh responded:

> We tested thee, and found thee wanting . . . Hadst thou been sincere in thy words, thou wouldst not have cast behind thy back the Book of God [the previous tablet] when it was

9. The caliphate is the office held by the caliph. It began with Abú-Bakr and, in the time of Bahá'u'lláh, was held by the sultan of Turkey. When the last Ottoman sultan, Muhammad VI, was deposed, the office of caliph lost its power and was abolished.

> sent unto thee by Him who is the Almighty, the All-Wise . . . For what thou hast done, thy kingdom shall be thrown into confusion, and thine empire pass from thy hands, as a punishment for what thou hast wrought. Bahá'u'lláh, in *The Promised Day Is Come*, p. 50.

The emperor soon was engulfed by catastrophe. In the greatest capitulation hitherto recorded by modern history, Napoleon's entire army surrendered at the Battle of Sedan (1870), and Napoleon was taken prisoner. The empire collapsed, a republic was proclaimed, and a bloody civil war ensued. The emperor's only son met death in the Zulu War. Eventually, the man who was the most powerful magnate on earth suffered an ignominious exile that lasted until his death.

In His tablet to the German Emperor, William (Wilhelm) I, Bahá'u'lláh warned him to consider the fate of Napoleon III, who had ignored the Call of God. Bahá'u'lláh asked,

> Do thou remember the one whose power transcended thy power [Napoleon III], and whose station excelled thy station. Where is he? Whither are gone the things he possessed? Take warning, and be not of them that are fast asleep. He it was who cast the tablet of God behind him, when We made known unto him what the hosts of tyranny had caused Us

> to suffer. Wherefore, disgrace assailed him from all sides, and he went down to dust in great loss. Think deeply, O King, concerning him, and concerning them who, like unto thee, have conquered cities and ruled over men. The All-Merciful brought them down from their palaces to their graves. Be warned, be of them who reflect. Bahá'u'lláh, in *The Promised Day Is Come*, pp. 36-37.

With a vision that knew no boundaries of time, the Author of that same tablet ominously forecast Germany's future transgressions, and her defeat as nations would rise up against her misdeeds. The tablet continues:

> O banks of the Rhine! We have seen you covered with gore, inasmuch as the swords of retribution were drawn against you; and you shall have another turn. And We hear the lamentation of Berlin, though she be today in conspicuous glory. Bahá'u'lláh, in *The Promised Day Is Come*, p. 37.

History more than adequately reveals the consequence of the German monarch's failure to heed the Voice of God. If the monarch had listened, would there have been a World War I, and "another turn," a World War II? Would there have been the divided city of Berlin?

Similarly, the Czar of Russia failed to respond to his tablet. Without divine guidance and oblivious of the call of God, he launched into a reactionary policy which caused widespread disillusionment, gave rise to nihilism, and ushered in a period of terrorist violence. Eventually, his disastrous reign culminated in his assassination. Bahá'u'lláh had foretold the judgment of God against him.

The emperor of Austria, Francis Joseph, visited Jerusalem while Bahá'u'lláh was imprisoned in 'Akká, a short journey away. Bahá'u'lláh warned him to hearken to the Call of God so near him, but he did not. Perhaps confident in a family rule that had lasted for almost five centuries, he ignored the force of reform and sought to reestablished old abuses, ignore the rights of nationalities, and restore bureaucratic centralization. In the end, his policies brought widespread turmoil and unrest which targeted their energies upon him and his family. His brother Maximilian was shot in Mexico. Crown Prince Rudolph perished in a dishonorable affair. The empress was assassinated in Geneva. Archduke Francis Ferdinand and his wife were murdered in Sarajevo, kindling a war in the midst of which the emperor himself died. Such was the fierce judgment of God against those who were called to come to the wedding feast but who did not respond.

Queen Victoria also received a tablet. It is said that the queen replied, "If this is of God, it will endure; if not, it can do no harm."[10] This is a slight variant of the

10. Shoghi Effendi, *The Promised Day is Come*, p. 65.

"Gamaliel test" of Acts 5:38-39. Queen Victoria stands in a different category from the others discussed for the simple reason that Bahá'u'lláh praised some of the reforms she introduced. He also praised the representative form of government which England adopted. The queen, having thus earned the praise of her Lord, enjoyed the longest reign of any British monarch. Queen Marie of Rumania, who became a Bahá'í, was a granddaughter of Queen Victoria.

The leaders of America (both North and South) also were addressed by Bahá'u'lláh. In His Most Holy Book (the Kitáb-i Aqdas), there appears a call for the rulers of the Americas to become champions of justice. The verses read:

> Hearken ye, O Rulers of America and the Presidents of the republics therein, unto that which the Dove is warbling on the Branch of Eternity: There is none other God but Me, the Ever-Abiding, the Forgiving, The All-Bountiful. Adorn ye the temple of dominion with the ornament of justice and of the fear of God, and its head with the crown of the remembrance of your Lord, the creator of the heavens. Thus counseleth you He Who is the Day-Spring of Names, as bidden by Him Who is the All-Knowing, the All-Wise. The Promised One hath appeared in this glorified Station, whereat all beings, both seen and unseen, have rejoiced. Take ye advantage of

> the day of God. Verily, to meet Him is better for you than all that whereon the sun shineth, could ye but know it. O concourse of rulers! Give ear unto that which hath been raised from the Dayspring of Grandeur: Verily, there is none other God but Me, the Lord of Utterance, the All-Knowing. Bind ye the broken with the hands of justice, and crush the oppressor who flourisheth with the rod of the commandments of your Lord, the Ordainer, the All-Wise. Bahá'u'lláh, in *The Proclamation of Bahá'u'lláh*, p. 61.

Finally, let us look at the tablet to Pope Pius IX. The wording is significant to those who are familiar with Christian prophecy. The tablet reads:

> O Pope! Rend the veils asunder. He Who is the Lord of Lords is come overshadowed with clouds, and the decree hath been fulfilled by God, the Almighty, the Unrestrained . . . He, verily, hath again come down from Heaven even as He came down from it the first time. Beware that thou disputest not with Him even as the Pharisees disputed with Him [Jesus] without a clear token or proof. On His right hand flow the living waters of grace, and on His left the choice Wine of justice, whilst before Him march the angels of Paradise,

bearing the banners of His signs. Beware lest any name debar thee from God, the Creator of earth and heaven. Leave thou the world behind thee, and turn towards thy Lord, through Whom the whole earth hath been illumined . . . Dwellest thou in palaces whilst He Who is the King of Revelation liveth in the most desolate of abodes? Leave them unto such as desire them, and set thy face with joy and delight towards the Kingdom . . . Arise in the name of thy Lord, the God of Mercy, amidst the peoples of the earth, and seize thou the Cup of Life with the hands of confidence, and first drink thou therefrom, and proffer it then to such as turn towards it amongst the peoples of all faiths . . . The Word which the Son concealed is made manifest. It hath been sent down in the form of a human temple in this day. Blessed be the Lord Who is the Father! He, verily, is come unto the nations in His most great majesty. Turn your faces towards Him, O concourse of the righteous!

O Supreme Pontiff! Incline thine ear unto that which the Fashioner of mouldering bones counseleth thee, as voiced by Him Who is His Most Great Name. Sell all the embellished ornaments thou dost possess, and expend them in the path of God . . . Verily, the day of ingathering is come, and all things have been separated from each other. He hath stored away that which He chose in the ves-

> sel of justice, and cast into fire that which befitteth it. Thus hath it been decreed by your Lord, the Mighty, the Loving, in this promised Day. He, verily, ordaineth what He pleaseth. There is none other God save He, the Almighty, the All-Compelling.
> Baha'u'lláh, in *The Proclamation of Bahá'u'lláh*, p. 83.

What happened to this papal monarch, who proclaimed the doctrine of the immaculate conception of the Virgin Mary (1854) and promulgated the teaching of papal infallibility (1870)? In the end he, too, suffered humiliation. In the very year he declared himself infallible, the troops of King Victor Emmanuel II of Italy entered Vatican City, over which popes had ruled by unchallengeable right for ten centuries, and imprisoned its pope, thereby signifying the permanent dismemberment of the papal empire. The papacy and its doctrines never have been the same.

The tablets of Bahá'u'lláh were not confined to singular rulers. Tablets also were addressed collectively to rulers, to clergy of many faiths, and to elected representatives in every land.

As a consequence of their misuses of power, Bahá'u'lláh boldly proclaimed, "From two ranks amongst men hath power been seized: kings and ecclesiastics."[11] If kings and ecclesiastics are the stars to which we turn

11. Shoghi Effendi, *The Promised Day is Come*, p. 20.

for guidance, have they fallen from the heaven of power and authority which they once enjoyed? The answer is obvious. The modern decline of kings and ecclesiastics is not accidental. It is in preparation to receive a new system of guidance, a new heaven over a new earth.

It is important to note that the fall of luminaries is not confined to heads of church and state. As the Bahá'í writings make plain, we all are guilty of both sins of commission and omission.[12] Many below the rank of king, pontiff, or caliph have actively opposed the Chosen One of God. Most of us have merely ignored Him. The sun, moon, and stars of the oppressors have and will be brought down quickly. The illuminating ability of the ignorant will survive only to the degree that they unconsciously do the will of God. As scripture and justice demand, the eclipse of the light of the sun and moon, and the fall of the stars, must continue until we rely no more on their light. The Bible makes clear that the Day is coming when the light from these luminaries will be needed no more because the Lord of Hosts will Himself provide Light.[13] We must only learn now to turn toward Him.

12. See Shoghi Effendi, *The Promised Day is Come*, p. 115.

13. "Then the moon shall be confounded, and the sun ashamed, when the Lord of hosts shall reign in Mount Zion, and in Jerusalem, and before his ancients gloriously." *Isaiah 24:23*. See also *Matthew 24* and *Revelation 21*.

A Literal Star-Fall Too

For those who enjoy literal interpretations of prophecy, we note that as Bahá'u'lláh wrote to the earthly luminaries announcing their downfall, the world experienced a star-fall in the physical heavens that has perhaps no parallel in recorded history. The event of the falling stars occurred on November 14, 1866, as Bahá'u'lláh was in European Turkey (Adrianople) writing the kings and rulers of the world. It consisted of a spectacular shower of meteors, by some accounts tens of thousands, which flashed for many hours across the night sky, falling from East to West all across Europe. The event was recorded in newspapers throughout the world.[14]

14. See Appendix 1 of A. Taherzadeh, *The Revelation of Bahá'u'lláh*, Vol. 2 (Oxford:George Ronald, 1983).

THE SEVENTH SEAL IS OPENED
(*Revelation 8:1-13*)

Chapter 12

THE WAY OF PILGRIMS

On August 31, 1868, Bahá'u'lláh arrived as a prisoner in Turkish Palestine, the land that was to become Israel. The Promised One had been led to His spiritual home. His arrival coincided with the beginning of great waves of Jewish immigration, that had been made possible by the signing of the Edicts of Toleration by the Turkish government. The land that God had promised the seed of Abraham, was being restored to meet its scriptural destiny.[1] Bahá'u'lláh was a descendant of Abraham's third wife, Katurah.

The city of 'Akká, known in Old Testament times as Acco (or Accho), was flanked by what we know today as Lebanon to the immediate north, with the plain of Sharon and Mount Carmel to the immediate south. The future significance of Carmel and Sharon were heralded with these words in the Old Testament:[2]

1. For example, *Genesis 12:1-3; 26:1-5; 28:13-15.*

2. Similarly, *Isaiah 65:10-11* reads: "And Sharon shall be a fold of flocks, and the valley of Achor, a place for the herds to lie down in, for my people that have sought me. But ye [the sinful] are they that forsake the Lord, that forget my holy mountain." While the vale of Achor is on the northwestern coast of the Dead Sea

> The wilderness and the solitary place shall be glad for them; and the desert shall rejoice, and blossom like the rose. It shall blossom abundantly, and rejoice even with joy and singing; the glory of Lebanon shall be given unto it, *the excellency of Carmel and Sharon; they shall see the Glory of the Lord*, and the excellency of our God . . . *And a highway shall be there, and a way, and it shall be called the way of holiness*; the unclean shall not pass over it, but it shall be for those, the wayfaring men, though fools shall not err therein. No lion shall be there, nor any ravenous beast shall go up thereon; it shall not be found there, but the redeemed shall walk there. And the ransomed of the Lord shall return, and to come to Zion with songs and everlasting joy upon their heads. *Isaiah 35:2-10* (Emphasis mine.)

Thus it was foretold that Carmel and Sharon were to see the Glory of the Lord, Bahá'u'lláh, and become a

(southern Israel), the reference may have meant Acco, as it is 'Akká that is near Sharon. The Book of Hosea (2:15) also mentions the valley of Achor, which the Guardian applies to 'Akká—See Shoghi Effendi, *God Passes By*, p. 184. If Acco, modern 'Akká, was not intended by the original writer, then the quotation probably would have to refer to all of Israel. Sharon, however, certainly applies to the Plain of Sharon at Carmel, and thus it is consistent to think of Achor as 'Akká.

way of holiness, a place for pilgrims, for the ransomed of the Lord.

Before Bahá'u'lláh arrived in 'Akká, the populace had been warned that a dangerous criminal was approaching with whom they were not to make contact. Bahá'u'lláh, sixty-four other Bahá'ís, and two followers of a sect that was antagonistic to Bahá'u'lláh were confined, by order of the Ottoman emperor, to perpetual banishment and strict incarceration in 'Akká. In addition, the Persian ambassador to Istanbul played an active role in maintaining the confinement of this dreaded Prisoner. He wrote to his government as follows:

> I have issued telegraphic and written instructions, forbidding that He (Bahá'u'lláh) associate with any one except His wives and children, or leave under any circumstances, the house wherein He is imprisoned. 'Abbás-Qulí Khán, the Consul-General in Damascus . . . I have three days ago, sent back, instructing him to proceed direct to 'Akká . . . confer with its governor regarding all necessary measures for the strict maintenance of their imprisonment . . . and appoint, before his return to Damascus, a representative on the spot to ensure that the orders issued by the Sublime Porte [Ottoman emperor] will, in no wise, be disobeyed. I have likewise, instructed him that once every three months he should proceed from Damascus to 'Akká, and personally watch over them, and submit his report to the Legation.[3]

3. Shoghi Effendi, *God Passes By*, p. 186.

Such was the severity and such were the precautions that two monarchs took to maintain the imprisonment of Bahá'u'lláh.

Bahá'u'lláh and His family were forbidden to associate with any of the other exiles or with other inhabitants of the city. They were confined to a citadel in the center of town which was surrounded by a moat of waste-water. Access to them was strictly regulated. Shortly after arriving in this most desolate of prisons, all fell ill. Three died.

After two years and two months Bahá'u'lláh and His family were moved to other quarters within the prison city. The government had other needs for the citadel. The family lived in four different houses within a year. In one of the houses, thirteen people of both sexes were forced to share one room. Yet there was more freedom than in the citadel, and Bahá'u'lláh now had access to the streets and residences of the prison city.

In time, the precautions of two kings were to prove of no avail. A Christian who had a wall built to reinforce the separation between his living space and that of Bahá'u'lláh tore down his wall and placed the enlarged house at the disposal of Bahá'u'lláh. The new governor of 'Akká became so enamored of the eldest son of Bahá'u'lláh, 'Abdu'l-Bahá, that he would remove his shoes in His presence and would send his own son to 'Abdu'l-Bahá for advice and counsel. Eventually, the governor sought permission to meet the Glory of God; the captor sought permission to meet his Prisoner. The governor went before Bahá'u'lláh humbly and silently and asked permission to serve Him.[4] Bahá'u'lláh asked the governor to repair the city aqueduct which had been in disuse for thirty years. The governor immediately complied. He also gathered all the writings of Bahá'u'lláh which came into his possession and had them recopied in the best calligraphic style. Such is the love and dedication which the Manifestation of God evoked even among those charged with persecuting Him.

Technically Bahá'u'lláh was a prisoner in what is now Israel until the end of His life. Although the restrictions placed on Him were relaxed, either by the growing love of those who held local office or through the inability of any enemy to enforce them, they were never canceled. Some nine years after the beginning of His incarceration in 'Akká, the then mufti (expounder of Muslim law) of the city, went before Bahá'u'lláh. While on his knees, he took the hand of Bahá'u'lláh, kissed it, and begged Him to leave that city, saying that no one would stop Him. Bahá'u'lláh refused to go without the permission of the state. The laws of the Bahá'í Revelation demand obedience to the laws of the country in which one resides, even if the laws are unjust, and Bahá'u'lláh kept the laws of His own Revelation. The mufti, who begged for a solid hour, assured Him that it was the wish of the people of 'Akká that He be granted freedom to take up residence outside the

4. Balyuzi, *Bahá'u'lláh the King of Glory* (Oxford: George Ronald) pp. 333-35.

city, where it was more pleasant. Technically, Bahá'u'lláh still could be considered a prisoner even outside the city. The next day a most amazing thing happened. Bahá'u'lláh, Prisoner of the Ottoman empire, was driven out of the city gate, past the guards, to a country residence which had been prepared for Him. No one made any objection. The majority of people had come to love Him and attributed many miracles to His presence.

Bahá'u'lláh lived in a place called Mazrá'ih, some ten miles north of 'Akká, for two years. He then moved to a deserted mansion called Bahjí, closer to 'Akká. It was at Bahjí that Bahá'u'lláh revealed a fuller measure of His transcendental sovereignty to the pilgrims who had come to drink of the wine of His presence and lay their lives in His hands. It was here, beside the Mountain of God (Mt. Carmel), in a mansion obtained for Him, that many could see that, far from being defeated, Bahá'u'lláh in fact had conquered all who opposed Him. It was here that Bahá'u'lláh filled to overflowing the cup of the hearts of the sincere ones, and here that He sent away those who were unworthy to meet Him, despite their rank.

As in the times of Jesus, most of the sincere ones were of humble origin. There is a wonderful story told by one of the pilgrims, which illustrates the experience of meeting Bahá'u'lláh at this time:

> The following day [after our arrival in 'Akká] we were summoned to the presence of the Blessed Beauty [Bahá'u'lláh]. God is my witness as to our

> state and condition at that time. A flood of tears was flowing from our eyes as we beheld His countenance. . . . The eyes of His bountiful favours were often directed toward us . . . One day we were summoned at the time of revelation and heard the melodies of holiness. Gracious God! at such a time not only was the soul exhilarated, but it seemed as if even the door, the walls, the trees, and the fruits were made to vibrate with the excitement. The Blessed Beauty was seated upon the throne of utterance, the verses of God were pouring out as a copious rain and the shrill voice of the Pen of the Most High could be heard. Each day we received our portion of the bounties from his presence and were in the utmost joy.[5]

This same pilgrim goes on to relate a story that closely echoes the parable of the wedding feast of the king's son:[6]

> One day Bahá'u'lláh informed my father that he would be visiting us in the afternoon. That day He arrived with a few of His disciples. We were both highly honoured by His presence and immersed in the ocean of His grace and bounties. After some time He arose to depart. We accompanied Him to the door and as He went out, he signalled to us not to accompany Him further. I watched from behind His grace-

5. A. Taherzadeh, *The Revelation of Bahá'u'lláh*, Vol. 3, pp. 160-161.
6. *Matthew 22:1-14*, cited in Chapter 2.

ful stature and the majesty of His walk, until He disappeared from my sight. I was so carried away, in this state I said to myself: What a pity! If only the kings of the world could recognize Him and arise to serve Him, both the Cause and the believers would be exalted in this day.

The following day when we attained His presence, He turned His face to me and addressed the following words to me with infinite charm and loving kindness. He said: "If the kings and rulers of the world had embraced the faith in this day, you people could never have found an entry into this exalted Court. You could never have had the opportunity to attain Our presence, nor could you ever have acquired the privilege of hearing the words of the Lord of Mankind. Of course the time will come when the kings and rulers of the world will become believers, and the Cause of God will be glorified outwardly. But this will happen after the meek and the lowly ones of the earth have won this inestimable bounty.

Contrast this story of a humble man meeting with Bahá'u'lláh to the account of two proud men who desired to meet Him. These two were the governor of 'Akká and a European general.[7] Their request for a meeting was denied, and they were requested to refer their concerns to 'Abdu'l-Bahá, the eldest son of

7. Taherzadeh, *The Revelation of Bahá'u'lláh*, Vol. 3, pp. 249-250.

Bahá'u'lláh, who typically dealt with all matters concerning the government. In the end, however, a rumor that Bahá'u'lláh was not even at the mansion, and therefore could not be a prisoner, required the governor to investigate. Permission was granted for the two men to visit.

As the officials drew near Bahá'u'lláh's chamber, they suddenly felt compelled to kneel at His threshold. It must have been some sight. The European general was a very large man, and together with the governor they must have completely filled the doorway. Bahá'u'lláh indicated there were seats on which they could sit, yet these two great men felt powerless to move. They sat in complete silence for about ten minutes, and as Bahá'u'lláh had nothing to say to them, the silence was unbroken. They then begged permission to leave, and it was granted. Humbly, they retreated. Such was the effect of Bahá'u'lláh on proud men.

The Covenant

The Ministry of Bahá'u'lláh lasted forty years. Before He ascended from this earthly plane, He prepared His followers for a priceless gift: a continuing Covenant between God and humankind. The Book of Revelation spoke of this Covenant, which would be established after the seventh angel's sounding. The verse reads:

> And the temple of God was opened in heaven, and there was seen in his temple the ark of his covenant; and there were lightnings, and voices, and thunderclaps, and an earthquake, and great hail. *Revelation 11:19*

If we recall that the temple of God can refer to the body of the Chosen One, we see that the ark of the covenant comes, as the Son comes from the Father, from the body of the Promised One. Prior to His passing, Bahá'u'lláh chose His eldest son, 'Abdu'l-Bahá, to be the only authorized Interpreter of the Word of God. As the verses indicated, this choice was made in the heaven of God's will. The signs—lightning, voices, thunder, earthquake, and hail—mark the grievous tests that befell those who opposed the continuation of the Faith of Bahá'u'lláh.

'Abdu'l-Bahá would resolve all conflicts, issues, and disputes within the Bahá'í community. He also would represent, defend, and organize the proclamation of the Faith after the passing of Bahá'u'lláh. All who turned to Him would be saved, all who disputed would be lost. He is, to Bahá'ís, the only true Exemplar of the Faith of Bahá'u'lláh. There could be no book long enough to extol His virtues.

When Bahá'u'lláh passed away in 1892, one of His disciples wrote:

> Methinks, the spiritual commotion set up in the world of dust had caused the worlds of God to trem-

> ble . . . My inner and outer tongue are powerless to portray the condition we were in . . . In the midst of the prevailing confusion a multitude of the inhabitants of 'Akká and of neighboring villages, that thronged the fields surrounding the Mansion [Bahjí], could be seen weeping, beating upon their heads, and crying aloud their grief.[8]

The same disciple was soon so distraught that he could not control his grief, and he drowned himself in the sea.

The commotion was even greater in Iran. It was 'Abdu'l-Bahá, still technically a prisoner of the Ottoman empire, who arose with superhuman strength to revivify the Bahá'ís and lead them in carrying the Message of His Father into distant lands. Bahá'u'lláh wrote long tablet concerning His son which reads in part:

> Render thanks unto God, O people, for His appearance; for verily He is the most great Favor unto you, the most perfect bounty upon you; and through Him every moldering bone is quickened. Whoso turneth towards Him hath turned towards God, and whoso turneth away from Him hath turned away from My Beauty, hath repudiated My Proof, and transgressed against Me. He is the Trust of God amongst you, His charge with you, His manifestation unto you and His appear-

8. Balyuzi, *Bahá'u'lláh The King of Glory*, p. 428.

> ance among His favored servants . . . We have sent Him down in the form of a human temple. Blest and sanctified be God Who createth whatsoever He willeth through His inviolable, His infallible decree. They who deprive themselves of the shadow of the Branch ['Abdu'l-Bahá], are lost in the wilderness of error, are consumed by the heat of worldly desires, and are of those who will assuredly perish.
> Bahá'u'lláh, in *The World Order of Bahá'u'lláh*, p. 135.

Thus 'Abdu'l-Bahá holds a place unique in religious history. He is not merely the favored disciple, as Peter was to Christ. His station is closer to that which 'Alí was given by Muḥammad. But even this analogy is not exact, as 'Alí was not destined to assume the reins of Muḥammad's religion immediately. Rather, 'Abdu'l-Bahá was God's gift to humankind, that the Faith of Bahá'u'lláh might accomplish its mission. Thus, the words and writings of 'Abdu'l-Bahá are sacred to Bahá'ís because of the unique station conferred upon Him by Bahá'u'lláh. Yet, as the Guardian of the Bahá'í Faith has explained, His Words are not equal in rank to those of Bahá'u'lláh although they are of equal validity.[9] 'Abdu'l-Bahá was not a Prophet, although He reflected perfectly the light of the Prophet in a way no ordinary human could match. He was the Inter-

9. Shoghi Effendi, *The World Order of Bahá'u'lláh*, p. 139.

preter of the Word of God and the Exemplar of the Faith revealed by Bahá'u'lláh.[10]

The Guardian of the Bahá'í Faith, whose writings I have quoted, is 'Abdu'l-Bahá's grandson, Shoghi Effendi. It was to him that the Bahá'í world turned (according to the explicit instructions of the Will and Testament of 'Abdu'l-Bahá) when 'Abdu'l-Bahá died in 1921. The Guardian's writings are considered not sacred, but authoritative. All questions were to be referred to him.

The Guardian died in 1957. Until the institution which Bahá'u'lláh established to rule the Bahá'í world, the Universal House of Justice, could be elected, the

10. A more complete statement of 'Abdu'l-Bahá's station is found in the writings of the Guardian: "He is, and should for all time be regarded, first and foremost, as the Center and Pivot of Bahá'u'lláh's peerless and all-enfolding Covenant, His most exalted handiwork, the stainless Mirror of His light, the perfect Exemplar of His teachings, the unerring Interpreter of His Word, the embodiment of every Bahá'í ideal, the incarnation of every Bahá'í virtue, the Most Mighty Branch sprung from the Ancient Root, the Limb of the Law of God, the Being 'round whom all names revolve,' the Mainspring of the Oneness of Humanity, the Ensign of the Most Great Peace, the Moon of the Central Orb of this most holy Dispensation—styles and titles that are implicit and find their truest, their highest and fairest expression in the magic name 'Abdu'l-Bahá. He is, above and beyond these appellations, the 'Mystery of God'—an expression by which Bahá'u'lláh Himself has chosen to designate Him, and which, while it does not by any means justify us to assign to Him the station of Prophethood, indicates how in the person of 'Abdu'l-Bahá the incomparable characteristics of a human nature and superhuman knowledge and perfection have been blended and are completely harmonized." Shoghi Effendi, *God Passes By*, p. 134.

affairs of the Cause were administered by men and women who had been designated "Hands of the Cause of God" by the Guardian.

In 1963, the first Universal House of Justice was elected by all the national Bahá'í institutions. This long-awaited date is the end point for the verse in Daniel (12:12) which reads: "Blessed is he that waiteth, and cometh to the thousand three hundred and five and thirty days." The three sets of days in Daniel—1,260, 1,290, and 1,335—are marked at their beginning and end by similar events. The 1,260 days are marked at beginning and end by the beginnings of two calendars: the Islamic and the Bahá'í. The 1,290 days are marked by two proclamations: Muḥammad's and Bahá'u'lláh's. The 1,335 days are marked by events that represent triumphs for the young Faiths: The beginning point of the prophecy most likely is the truce of al-Hudaybiyyah in Mecca; the ending point is firmly fixed in 1963 with the election of the Bahá'í Universal House of Justice.[11]

11. Bahá'í writings specify the end-point as 1963, a century after the proclamation of Bahá'u'lláh. 'Abdu'l-Bahá wrote, "These days must be reckoned as solar and not lunar years. For according to this calculation a century will have elapsed from the dawn of the Sun of Truth, then will the teachings of God be firmly established upon the earth, and the Divine Light shall flood the world from the East even unto the West." (Helen Hornby, *Lights of Guidance*, New Delhi: Bahá'í Publishing Trust, 1983, p. 324.) Shoghi Effendi clearly affirms that the end date refers to 1963. (*Lights of Guidance*, p. 324.) Counting backward 1,335 solar years, as specified, yields the date 628 A.D. This was the date of the truce which performed the similar function of granting an institutional basis to Islam.

The seat of the Universal House of Justice is on Mount Carmel. This is the administrative center of the Bahá'í world. To Bahá'ís, this institution represents the fulfillment of the prophecy found in Isaiah:

> And it shall come to pass in the last days, *that the mountain of the Lord's House shall be established in the top of the mountains*, and shall be exalted above the hills; and all nations shall flow unto it. *Isaiah 2:2* (Emphasis mine.)

The Universal House of Justice is the Lord's House, to which the nations will turn for justice. The Bahá'í institutions—of which the Universal House of Justice is the head—are, in the words of the Guardian, "the sole refuge of a civilization in the embrace of doom."[12]

Every year, thousands of Bahá'í pilgrims take up the way of holiness spoken of in the beginning of this chapter and visit the shrines of the Bahá'í Faith on Mt. Carmel, Sharon, and 'Akká.

12. Shoghi Effendi, *The Promised Day is Come*, p. 17.

THE BEAST IS BOUND
for one thousand years. (*Revelation 20:1-15*)

Chapter 13

THE BEAST, BABYLON AND THE PROMISED ONE

In the concluding chapters of the Book of Revelation, all events center around three main characters: the beast, Babylon, and the Promised One. These concluding chapters contradict the idea of the Lord returning on physical clouds, instantly dispensing judgment and making all things in the world right. Instead, they tell of opposition to the Promised One. Chapter 19 of the Book of Revelation, which recounts the coming of the Lord, reads:

> And I saw heaven opened and, behold, a white horse; and he that sat upon him was called Faithful and True, and in righteousness he doth judge and make war. His eyes were like a flame of fire, and on his head were many crowns; and he had a name written, that no man knew, but he himself. And he was clothed with a vesture dipped in blood; and his name is called The Word of God. And the armies that were in heaven followed him

> upon white horses, clothed in fine linen, white and clean. And out of his mouth goeth a sharp sword, that with it he should smite the nations, and he shall rule them with a rod of iron; and he treadeth the winepress of the fierceness and wrath of Almighty God. And he hath on his vesture and on his thigh a name written, KING OF KINGS, AND LORD OF LORDS. And I saw an angel standing in the sun; and he cried with a loud voice, saying to all the fowls that fly in the midst of heaven, Come and gather yourselves together unto the supper of the great God, That ye may eat the flesh of kings, and the flesh of captains, and the flesh of mighty men, and the flesh of horses and of them that sit on them, and the flesh of all men, both free and enslaved, both small and great. *And I saw the beast, and the kings of the earth, and their armies, gathered together to make war against him* that sat on the horse, and against his army. *Revelation 19:11-19* (Emphasis mine.)

If the Lord returned on physical clouds, what king or army would argue with Him?[1] The literal vision of

1. Bahá'u'lláh writes, "Were Jesus, Son of Mary, accompanied by angels, to descend from the visible heaven upon the clouds; who would dare to disbelieve, who would dare to reject the truth, and wax Disdainful?" *The Kitáb-i-Íqán*, p. 81.

the Lord coming on clouds thus is defeated by the Bible itself. But why would the kings and their armies be angry when the Lord comes? Because the Promised One comes to claim His Kingdom on earth.[2] The Promised One, as Paul informs us, has come to take all authority. In I Corinthians 15:24, Paul writes, "Then cometh the end, when he shall have delivered up the kingdom to God, even the Father, when he shall have put down all rule and all authority and power."

As we have seen, Bahá'u'lláh made plain in countless tablets His claim to be the Promised One, the Voice of God, and the King of kings. The prophecy thus finds its first fulfillment in the actions of the rulers of the region who rose up against Bahá'u'lláh: the Shah of Persia and the Sultan of Turkey. History has recorded God's judgment against these kings. But the battle against the Promised One is far from over.

2. For example, in *Revelation 11:15-18*: "And the seventh angel sounded; and there were great voices in heaven, saying, *The kingdom of this world is become the kingdom of our Lord, and of his Christ*, and he shall reign forever and ever. And the four and twenty elders, who sat before God on their thrones, fell upon their faces, and worshiped God, Saying, We give thee thanks, O Lord God Almighty, who art, and wast, and art to come, because thou hast taken to thee thy great power, and hast reigned. *And the nations were angry and thy wrath is come*, and the time of the dead, that they should be judged, and that thou shouldest give reward unto thy servants, the prophets, and to the saints, and them that fear thy name, small and great, and shouldest destroy them who destroy the earth." (Emphasis mine.)

The New Beast

Often in the Bible, the beast is used as a symbol for a specific kingdom or empire. We identified the beast in Chapter 11 and the dragon in Chapter 12 of the Book of Revelation as the Umayyad Dynasty of the Islamic empire. This beast had seven heads (that is, it stretched over the entire Old World) and ten horns (the names of its rulers).[3] The members of this dynasty interfered with the work of Muḥammad and 'Alí, and harassed and killed many of their descendants.

3. *Revelation 17:8-13* also supplies information about the Beast. The text reads, "The beast that thou sawest was, and is not, and shall ascend out of the bottomless pit, and go into perdition; and they that dwell on the earth shall wonder, whose names were not written in the book of life from the foundation of the world, when they behold the beast that was, and is not, and yet is. And here is the mind which hath wisdom. The seven heads are seven mountains, on which the woman sitteth. And there are seven kings: five are fallen, and one is, and the other is not yet come; and when he cometh, he must continue a short space. And the beast that was, and is not, even he is the eighth, and is of the seven, and goeth into perdition. And the ten horns which thou sawest are ten kings, who have received no kingdom as yet, but receive power as kings one hour with the beast. These have one mind, and shall give their power and strength unto the beast." In short, the heads are empires of the Old World, over which kings rule. The five which had passed in the time of the writer would have been Egypt, Babylonia, Assyria, Persia, and Greece. The one that is (at the time of the writer) was Roman. The one yet to come, was Byzantium. The one next to come, with ten rulers is the Umayyad or early Islamic dynasty, which ruled the same lands as the previously mentioned empires (hence, it is an eighth empire but of the seven and has the seven regions mentioned by 'Abdu'l-Bahá). The rulers of this last empire were leagued with the beast.

But there are *two* beasts in Chapter 13 of the Book of Revelation. In all probability, the first beast is the Umayyad dynasty. It has seven heads and ten horns as did the Umayyad dragon of Chapter 12. The transition from dragon to beast may represent merely the transition from a personal to an institutional manifestation of opposition to God's Messengers.

The second beast then appears in the image of the first:

> *And I beheld another beast* coming up out of the earth; and he had two horns like a lamb, and he spoke like a dragon. And he exerciseth all the power of the first beast before him, and causeth the earth and them who dwell on it to worship the first beast, whose deadly wound was healed. And he doeth great wonders, so that he maketh fire come down from heaven on the earth in the sight of men, And deceiveth them that dwell on the earth by the means of those miracles which he had power to do in the sight of the beast; saying to them that dwell on the earth, *that they should make an image to the beast*, which had the wound by a sword, and did live. And he hath power to give life unto the image of the beast, that the image of the beast should both speak, and cause that as many as would not worship the image of the beast should be killed. *Revelation 13:11-15* (Emphasis mine.)

Some Bahá'ís think that this second beast refers to the leaders who followed the Umayyads (e.g. the Abbasids or the caliphate in general), but this is conjecture. This second beast probably is still with us. Note that in the verses above the beast is not bound by the 1,260-year duration of Islam. He may, in fact, not have appeared until after the year 1260 A.H.

The Báb wrote in a tablet: "As to those who have put the kindred of 'Alí to death, *ere long* they shall realize to what depths of perdition they have descended" (Emphasis mine).[4] In another tablet He wrote: "Yazíd, the son of Mu'ávíyih, out of corrupt desire, bartered away the head of the true Joseph to the fiendish people for a trifling price and a petty sum for his property. Verily they repudiated God by committing a grievous error. *Erelong* will God wreak His vengeance upon them, at the time of our Return." (Emphasis mine.)[5] In both cases the Báb was speaking of a *future* punishment for those that *long ago* had harmed the descendants of Muḥammad and 'Alí. But the Báb was not speaking about those long dead; He was speaking about the *present* persecutors of His Faith. Both the Báb and Bahá'u'lláh indicated that the people who persecuted Muḥammad and 'Alí and their descendants were, in spirit, *the same people* who were persecuting them and their followers. The modern persecutors are, in the language of the Bible, "in the image" of the beast. The

4. *Selections from the Writings of the Báb*, p. 5.
5. *Selections from the Writings of the Báb*, p. 49.

beast is alive again, and has taken the lives of thousands of Bábís and Bahá'ís.

Is the beast dead? In its early form, the beast consisted of the kings and rulers of Persia and Turkey and their minions, who sought to exterminate the young faith of the Báb and Bahá'u'lláh. The clerical leaders were anxious to assert their authority and interpretations over that of the Promised Ones. In doing so, they became false prophets. As the parable of the Lord of the vineyard reminds us, the clergy that is charged with guiding the believers can often become the source of misguidance.[6] In the Dispensation of the Báb and Bahá'u'lláh, the Islamic clergy have been particularly beastly in their actions. Bahá'u'lláh writes of them:

> Were the eye to be anointed and illumined with the collyrium of the knowledge of God, it would surely discover *that a number of voracious beasts* have gathered and preyed upon the carrion of the souls of men. *The Kitáb-i-Íqán* p. 31. (Emphasis mine.)

6. "A certain man planted a vineyard, and leased it to tenants and went into a far country for a long time. And at the season he sent a servant to the tenants, that they should give him of the fruit of the vineyard; but the tenants beat him, and sent him away empty. And again he sent another servant; and they beat him also, and treated him shamefully, and sent him away empty. And again he sent a third; and they wounded him also, and cast him out. Then said the Lord of the vineyard, What shall I do? I will send

Perhaps, then, it is the clergy that is the beast. This fits particularly well, because the prophecy specifies that the beast has horns like a lamb but speaks like a dragon. Furthermore, in Islamic lands, it was the clergy who had control over people and government.

The persecution of Bahá'ís has not ended. It continues throughout all Islamic lands and is growing, in some forms, in the West. This persecution has interfered with all aspects of the lives of Bahá'ís, including (as the prophecy states) their rights to buy and sell. Pensions, property, savings, education, and, in hundreds of instances, life itself all have been taken from Bahá'ís in Iran and in other Islamic countries in recent times. In the West, denunciations of Bahá'ís from the pulpit, from television ministries, and from the press of the religious right continues, although most of these antagonists are ill-informed of Bahá'í beliefs. The beast then refers to the organized opponents of Bahá'u'lláh —initially the clergy and governments of the East, and perhaps one day including the ministries and governments of the West.

---

my beloved son; it may be they will reverence him when they see him. But the tenants saw him, they reasoned among themselves, saying, This is the heir. Come, let us kill him, that the inheritance may be ours. So they cast him out of the vineyard, and killed him. What therefore shall the Lord of the vineyard do unto them? He shall come and destroy these tenants, and shall give the vineyard to others." *Luke 20:9-16*

666

Chapter 13 of Revelation ends with the infamous prophecy of the 666, which, we are told, is the number of the beast and of a man. The verses read:

> Here is wisdom. Let him that hath understanding count the number of the beast; for it is the number of a man; and his number is *six hundred threescore and six. Revelation 13:18* (Emphasis mine.)

The verse is set off by the cryptic phrase, "Here is wisdom," thus introducing the possibility that this is a first-century interpretation of the preceding scripture which has been added by a scribe or scholar. In fact, there are two versions of the number given in ancient biblical texts. One set records the number 666; another the number 616. Both numbers can represent the name Nero Caesar when the name is rendered numerically by two variant spellings.[7] Nero Caesar was actively persecuting Christians when the Book of Revelation was written and copied. So the number may have been added as a later interpretation.

7. When Nero Caesar is spelled in Hebrew and the letters are given their numeric equivalent, the result (50 + 200 + 6 + 50 & 100 + 60 + 200) sums 666. If the final consonant in the Latin form of Nero is left off, the result sums (50 + 200 + 6 & 100 + 60 + 200) 616 (See Beckwith, *The Apocalypse of John*, pp. 404-405).

If the number was not an editorial addition, it still is not clear from the text whether the number refers to the first, the second, or both beasts in Revelation 13. Divergent interpretations have been given from Christian and Bahá'í scholars. The difficulty in fixing the beast's identity, however, may be simply that the man or institution has not yet appeared.

The 144,000

In the next verses, Revelation introduces a parenthetic expression about a hundred and forty-four thousand who would be saved:

> And I looked and, lo, a Lamb stood on Mount Zion, *and with him an hundred forty and four thousand* having his Father's name written in their foreheads. And I heard a voice from heaven, like the voice of many waters, and like the voice of a great thunder; and I heard the voice of harpers harping with their harps. *And they sang, as it were, a new song* before the throne, and before the four living creatures and the elders; and no man could learn that song but the hundred and forty and four thousand, who were redeemed from the earth. *Revelation 14:1-3* (Emphasis mine.)

The hundred and forty-four thousand have been identified in scripture as coming from the twelve tribes of Israel.[8] Thus, attempts to make them Christian, Muslim, or Bahá'í (except by conversion) probably are in error. But it is wrong to think we are talking about a literal hundred and forty-four thousand. The number clearly is symbolic, as is the number of tribes. In fact, the twelve tribes do not exist anymore. Ten of the tribes were carried off into exile by Sargon II in 722 B.C., and they vanished from history. Twelve is simply another biblical symbol for completeness, and a hundred and forty-four thousand is just twelve times twelve (times a thousand).

What, then, is the meaning of these verses? Recall that the first mention of the hundred and forty-four thousand was after the angel of the East appeared with the seal of the living God, both of which we related to Muḥammad.[9] This angel commanded that the earth, sea, and trees not be harmed until those who were sealed were gathered. But this period of gathering must be related to the length of the dispensation of Islam, which ended in the year 1844 (1260 A.H.). After this, we know the angels holding the winds of God's wrath are allowed to unleashed their fury.

Next we are told that one hundred and forty-four thousand appear on Mount Zion with a lamb, and that they have their Father's name on their foreheads. An

8. *Revelation 7:4-8.*
9. See Appendix 1.

explanation of these new symbols will help us. Mount Zion was the hill on which the temple was built. It represents the place of holiness and authority, a place from which holiness and authority issue. The lamb and other animals were used in sacrificial rites to purify the temple. But this lamb is special. He is a symbol for the Manifestation of God, God's ultimate sacrifice. At the end of the gathering, the verses say, the hour of judgment is come.[10] It is time now *to give glory to God*. This is the Father's name. Who, then, are the 144,000 who "follow the Lamb wherever he goeth" who are "the first fruits unto God and to the Lamb" and who are "without fault before the throne of God?"[11] Do we yet know?

The Book of Revelation tells of four victories: the victory of Christ and the early Christians; of Muḥammad, 'Alí, and the early Muslims; of the Báb and Bahá'u'lláh; and of the vindication and restoration of Israel. The Jews of at least some of the twelve tribes passed through each of these three religious epochs. In each epoch, some Jews found at least a portion of prophetic fulfillment. In each one, some "sang, as it were, a new song." Yet, for Jews collectively there has been no new heaven and earth. The verses that we are

10. Immediately after the description of the 144,000 we find: "And I saw another angel fly in the midst of heaven, having the everlasting gospel to preach unto them that dwell on the earth, and to every nation, and kindred, and tongue, and people, Saying with a loud voice, Fear God, and give glory to him; for the hour of his judgment is come; and worship him that made heaven, and earth, and the sea, and the fountains of waters." *Revelation 14:6-7.*

11. *Revelation 14:4.*

considering contain the promise of that new heaven and earth, first and foremost for the Jews. Therefore, I believe that the 144,000 symbolizes the complete reconciliation of Israel to the glorified Faith of the Father. When this occurs, *all* people will have found their new heaven and new earth.

The Babylon We Are In

The next verse in the Book of Revelation announces the hour of judgment and the fall of Babylon:

> And there followed another angel, saying, Babylon is fallen, that great city, because she made all nations drink of the wine of the wrath of her fornication. *Revelation 14:8*

As the Bible makes clear, Babylon is the symbolic home of the ungodly and materialistic. It is "the habitation of demons, and the hold of every foul spirit."[12] It is also worldwide. The Bible makes plain: "All nations have drunk of the wine of the wrath of her fornication, and the kings of the earth have committed fornication with her, and the merchants of the earth are grown rich through the abundance of her delicacies."[13] It is hard to escape the conclusion that most of the

12. *Revelation 18:2.*
13. *Revelation 18:3.*

modern world lives in Babylon. The Guardian of the Bahá'í Faith writes of the signs of our habitation:

> The signs of moral downfall, consequent to the dethronement of religion and the enthronement of these usurping idols are too numerous and too patent for even a superficial observer of the state of present-day society to notice. The spread of lawlessness, of drunkenness, of gambling, and of crime; the inordinate love of pleasure, of riches, and of other earthly vanities; the laxity in morals, revealing itself in the irresponsible attitude toward marriage, in the weakening of parental control, in the rising tide of divorce, in the deterioration in the standard of literature and of the press, and in the advocacy of theories that are the very negation of purity, of morality and chastity—these evidences of moral decadence, invading both the East and the West, permeating every stratum of society, and instilling their poison in its members of both sexes, young and old alike, blacken still further the scroll upon which are inscribed the manifold transgressions of an unrepentant humanity.[14]

The next verses of Revelation speak of the Son of man reaping the harvest of the earth—that is, gathering up those who will listen to the new message. There follows the last plagues to fall upon humankind, the seven bowls of wrath poured upon us because we have

14. Shoghi Effendi, *Promised Day Is Come*, p. 114-115.

not listened to God. The plagues fall upon men who worship the beast, upon the sea, upon the rivers, upon the sun, upon the throne of the beast, upon the Euphrates, and, finally, upon the air.[15] The calamities, it seems, are worldwide. We are living through them now.

Next it is announced that Babylon the harlot has fallen, and yet God still must plead with us to leave her:

> And I heard another voice from heaven, saying, *Come out of her, my people, that ye be not partakers of her sins*, and that ye receive not of her plagues; For her sins have reached unto heaven, and God hath remembered her iniquities. *Revelation 18:4-5* (Emphasis mine.)

Are we still in Babylon? It is difficult for us to know for sure, and even more difficult to know how to get out.

15. The seven bowls of wrath may follow the same pattern as seen elsewhere, a division of four and three. If so, the first four bowls may refer to background disasters from the time of Christ and the beast mentioned at the first bowl may be the beast that fought against Christianity, the Roman empire. The beast at the fifth bowl may then be the Umayyad beast. The sixth bowl makes way for the kings of the East and mentions this is the time when the Promised One appears like a thief. This can easily be related to the Ministry of the Báb, whose advent cleared the way for the final battle, and during whose Ministry, Bahá'u'lláh appeared like a thief in the night. The seventh bowl would represent the final battle of our time. However, all of this is speculative. The bowls may not relate to separate dispensations, but may all be reserved for our time.

These are serious problems. The Babylon of ungodliness and materialism has become so universal that we have lost most frames of reference outside of Babylon. Thus we are increasingly unable to see where we are. This may be especially true for our children, who know nothing but Babylon. But even if we are aware that we are in Babylon, can we escape? Which church, which doctrine, which light is strong enough to lead us to the New Jerusalem? Can this New Jerusalem be found without the Promised One?

The New Jerusalem

In the end, after the Promised One comes and the kings and nations of the earth war against Him and his followers, there is at last established a new heaven, a new earth, and a new Jerusalem.[16] The verses read:

> *And I saw a new heaven and a new earth* for the first heaven and the first earth were passed away, and there was no more sea. *And I, John, saw the holy city, new Jerusalem*, coming down from God out of heaven, prepared

16. Bahá'u'lláh explains that one of the meanings of a new heaven refers to a new Revelation and a new religion (*The Kitáb-i-Íqán*, p. 40, 44). A new earth is the response to that religion, a new earth of understanding (*The Kitáb-i-Íqán*, pp. 46-48). The New Jerusalem is the City of New Laws (*The Kitáb-i-Íqán*, pp. 196-99; *Epistle to the Son of the Wolf*, pp. 144-45).

> as a bride adorned for her husband. And I heard a great voice out of heaven saying, Behold, the tabernacle of God is with men, and he will dwell with them, and they shall be his people, and God himself shall be with them, and be their God. And God shall wipe away all tears from their eyes; and there shall be no more death, neither sorrow, nor crying, neither shall there be any more pain; for the former things are passed away. And he that sat upon the throne said, Behold, I make all things new. And he said unto me, Write; for these words are true and faithful. *Revelation 21:1-5* (Emphasis mine.)

In these verses and the ones that follow, the new Jerusalem is referred to as the bride of the Lamb. The city to which Jesus was wed was a redeemed Judaism. It was, as the next verses make plain, a city "having the glory of God."[17] It had gates "which are the names of the twelve tribes of the children of Israel" and foundations in which are "the names of the twelve apostles of the

17. "And there came unto me one of the seven angels who had the seven bowls full of the seven last plagues, and talked with me, saying, Come here, I will show the bride, the Lamb's wife. And he carried me away in Spirit to a great and high mountain, and showed me that great city, the holy Jerusalem, descending out of heaven from God, *having the glory of God*; and her light was like a stone most precious, even like a jasper stone, clear as crystal." *Revelation 21:9-11* (Emphasis mine.)

Lamb." It is interesting that the foundations are of Christianity and the gates are of Judaism, instead of the reverse. Perhaps the gates represent a return to Israel by the Jews, which continues to this day.

Let us think of the new Jerusalem as Israel herself. Bounded by the four walls of the compass and entered by the gates of Judaism, this new Jerusalem, the City of Peace, is the promised Holy Land not only for Jews but also for Christians, Muslims, and peoples of all faiths.[18] However, the city cannot be entered without acknowledging that it was built upon the foundations of Christianity. As the Guardian of the Bahá'í Faith makes plain, all accepting the Bahá'í Faith must acknowledge the divine character of Christianity.[19] It is through the suffering of Christ that the city was built. Bahá'u'lláh writes:

> Know thou that when the Son of Man yielded up His breath to God, the whole creation

18. While I have concentrated in this book on the prophecies of Christianity, Bahá'u'lláh claims to fulfill the prophecies of all true religions. Hence the followers of all religions find their fulfillment in Bahá'u'lláh and will consequently see Israel as their Holy Land.

19. "As to the position of Christianity, let it be stated without any hesitation or equivocation that its divine origin is unconditionally acknowledged, that the Sonship and Divinity of Jesus Christ are fearlessly asserted, that the divine inspiration of the Gospel is fully recognized, that the reality of the mystery of the Immaculacy of the Virgin Mary is confessed, and the primacy of Peter, Prince of the Apostles, is upheld and defended." Shoghi Effendi, *The Promised Day is Come*, p. 109.

> wept with a great weeping. By sacrificing Himself, however, a fresh capacity was infused into all created things. Its evidence, as witnessed in all the peoples of the earth, are now manifest before thee. *Gleanings from the Writings of Bahá'u'lláh*, p. 85.

Let us note, however, what happens when we enter into this city which Christ promised to Jews and all the peoples of the world. As we enter it through scripture, we note some differences with the Jerusalem of the past. There is neither a temple nor a Lamb to offer as sacrifice, as the next verses make plain:

> *And I saw no temple in it*; for the Lord God Almighty and the Lamb are the temple of it. And the city had no need of the sun, neither of the moon, to shine in it; *for the glory of God did light it*, and the Lamb is the lamp of it. *And the nations of them who are saved shall walk in the light of it*, and the kings of the earth do bring their glory and honor into it. *Revelation 21:22-24* (Emphasis mine.)

The Lamb is in heaven beside the throne of God, not in the city. There will be no giant statue of Jesus, no gargantuan crucifix to profane the new Jerusalem. The Lamb is in heaven, where we find that it is the Glory of God who has lit Him. No matter how much we adore the Lamb (Jesus), in the end we must see that it is not the Lamb with whom we must be primarily concerned. It is with the One who sits upon the throne of God. The Lamb, as scripture reminds us, has given up His Kingdom to the Father.[20] There can be no doubt that Bahá'u'lláh claims to be in the seat of the Father. He tells his followers:

> O wayfarer in the path of God! . . . Go forth with the Tablet of God and His signs, and rejoin them that have believed in Me, and announce unto them tidings of Our most holy Paradise. Warn, then, those that have joined partners with Him. Say: *I am come to you, O people, from the Throne of glory, the Most Powerful, the Most Exalted, the Most Great.* In mine hand I carry the testimony of God, your Lord and the Lord of your sires of old. Weigh it with the just Balance that ye possess, the Balance of the testimony of the Prophets and Messengers of God. *Gleanings from the Writings of Bahá'u'lláh*, p. 281.

Will the people weigh the message fairly?

The Revelation of Bahá'u'lláh has revealed a new heaven. In this boundless heaven there is room for the

20. *1 Corinthians 15:24* reads, "Then cometh the end when He shall have delivered up the kingdom to God, even the Father: when he shall have put down all authority and power."

light of the saints of Judaism and Christianity. There is room, too, for the light of the heroes and saints of Islam, of whom the Bible spoke. And there is room for the light of the heroes and saints of the Báb and Bahá'u'lláh, newly and continuously born into it. There no longer is room for those who think themselves partners with God. There no longer is room for fanaticism and intolerance. The new heavens are wide, and beneath them the earth can be reconstructed. It is an ancient promise that God will make of earth His footstool. Seated upon His throne, in a new heaven, He has set forth to do this.[21]

21. I wish to say a word about the Lamb. While I think it most natural, and in some places essential, to interpret the Lamb as Jesus in the Book of Revelation, there is a certain beauty in recognizing that the Lamb is a symbol of sacrifice and may therefore be applied to other sacrifices. More especially, I have in mind that the Lamb is a good symbol for every Manifestation of God. In the beginning of the Book of Revelation, the Lamb certainly is Jesus. It is His sacrifice, as both Revelation and Bahá'í writings remind us, that has brought us these prophecies and that has brought so much to the world. Later, however, the Lamb may refer to Muḥammad. Recall that Muḥammad too had 12 apostles, in the form of lineal descendants. Later still, after 1844, the Lamb who is slain may refer to the Báb—the return of Christ who stands beside the throne on Mount Zion. Finally, the Lamb may refer to the human station of Bahá'u'lláh, as He suffers as Manifestation of God, before the throne of God's command. None of this is, I feel, necessary. The Lamb can refer to Jesus throughout, and in no way should glory be taken from Him. Still, the symbol does invite other identifications which, I think, broaden our vision of all that has happened.

THE NEW JERUSALEM
". . . for the Glory of God did lighten it." (*Revelation 21:9-27*)

Chapter 14

THE SPIRIT OF OUR TIMES

Do we really need a new religion? Isn't our trouble that we haven't followed the teachings we have?

Questions like these miss the central point of my thesis: There really is only one religion, but it is progressive. The ministries of the three Chosen Ones of God since the time of Jesus all are part of the Bible. They are part of the unfolding story of God's destiny for humanity.

The final message of the Bible is that the Lord will come to establish His Kingdom on earth. Whether we read this message in Isaiah[1] or Micah,[2] in the Lord's prayer,[3] or in countless places in Revelation,[4] the inescapable conclusion is that we have been promised that

1. "In the last days, the mountain of the Lord's house shall be established in the top of the mountains, and shall be exalted above the hills; and all nations shall flow unto it." *Isaiah 2:2.*

2. "He [God] will settle disputes among the nations among the great powers near and far." *Micah 4:3.*

3. "Thy kingdom come, Thy will be done in earth as it is in heaven." *Matthew 6:10.*

4. For example, in *Revelation 15:4*, we read: "Who shall not fear thee, O lord, and glorify thy name? For thou alone art holy; for all nations shall come and worship before thee; for thy judgements are made manifest." And in *Revelation 19:16*, we find:

the Lord will come to establish international justice. He will come to reign as the King of kings,[5] and He will have on his head many crowns.[6]

In the Christian West we are used to thinking of Jesus as our shepherd.[7] Scripture, however, has promised us a time when a universal shepherd will appear: "And when the Chief Shepherd shall appear, ye shall receive a crown of glory that fadeth not away." (1 Peter 5:4) The work of a chief shepherd is to bring different herds together. The various nations and religions are these herds. Bringing them together, then, is the work of Bahá'u'lláh.

Very few Westerners ever met Bahá'u'lláh. One who did was Professor E. G. Browne of Cambridge University, who later recorded his impressions. During their meeting Bahá'u'lláh explained the central purpose of His Revelation. Browne wrote of his meeting:

> Though I dimly suspected whither I was going and whom I was to behold (for no intimation had been given to me), a second or two elapsed ere, with a throb of wonder and awe, I became definitely conscious that the room was not untenanted. In the

"And out of his [the Promised One's] mouth goeth a sharp sword, that with it he should smite the nations, and he shall rule them with a rod of iron; and he treadeth the winepress of the fierceness and wrath of Almighty God."

5. *Revelation 19:16.*
6. *Revelation 19:12.*
7. See *John 10:11.*

corner where the divan met the wall sat a wondrous and venerable figure, crowned with a felt head-dress of the kind called taj by dervishes (but of unusual height and make), round the base of which was wound a small white turban. The face of him on whom I gazed I can never forget, though I cannot describe it. Those piercing eyes seemed to read one's very soul; power and authority sat on that ample brow; while the deep lines on the forehead and face implied an age which the jet-black hair and beard flowing down in indistinguishable luxuriance almost to the waist seemed to belie. No need to ask in whose presence I stood, as I bowed myself before one who is the object of a devotion and love kings might envy and emperors sigh for in vain!

A mild dignified voice bade me be seated, and then continued:—"Praise be to God that thou hast attained! . . . Thou hast come to see a prisoner and an exile . . . We desire but the good of the world and the happiness of the nations; yet they deem us a stirrer up of sedition worthy of bondage and banishment . . . That all nations should become one in faith and all men as brothers; that the bonds of affection and unity between the sons of men should be strengthened; that diversity of religion should cease, and differences of race annulled—what harm is there in this? . . . Yet so it shall be; these fruitless strifes, these ruinous wars shall pass away, and the 'Most Great Peace' shall come . . . Do not you in Europe need this also? Is not this that which Christ foretold? . . . Yet do we see your kings and rulers lavishing their treasures more freely on means for the destruction of the human race than on that which would conduce to the happiness of mankind . . . These strifes and this bloodshed and discord must cease, and all men be as one kindred and one family . . . Let not a man glory in this, that he loves his country; let him glory in this, that he loves his kind . . ." Such, so far as I can recall them, were the words of Beha' [sic]. Let those who read them consider well with themselves whether such doctrines merit death and bonds, and whether the world is more likely to gain or lose by their diffusion.[8]

In countless epistles, Bahá'u'lláh repeated this central theme of His ministry. In one passage we read: "We, verily, have come to unite and weld together all that dwell on earth."[9] In another: "It is Our purpose, through the loving providence of God—exalted be His glory—and His surpassing mercy, to abolish through the force of Our utterance, all disputes, war, and bloodshed from the face of the earth."[10]

The message of Jesus was simple. He spoke of the victory of love, faith, and compassion over orthodoxy and the forces of negation. Christians have applied this positive force to save individuals from sin and from self. This work must continue. However, there is now

8. Quoted in *Bahá'u'lláh The King of Glory*, pp. 371-73.
9. Bahá'u'lláh, *Epistle to the Son of the Wolf*, p. 24.
10. Bahá'u'lláh, *Epistle to the Son of the Wolf*, p. 34.

a need to add to this work. Bahá'u'lláh writes in a tablet that begins, "O concourse of Christians!":

> Verily He [Jesus] said: "Come ye after Me, and I will make you to become fishers of men." In this day, however, We say: "Come ye after Me, that We may make you to become quickeners of mankind." *The Proclamation of Bahá'u'lláh*, p. 91.

It is no longer the individual only who needs saving. It is the body of humanity and the international relations of governments and peoples for whose salvation we must work. We need a new world order, a new set of operating principles that are easy to understand. We also need to look at issues globally. We must recognize that in our day our salvation, peace, and security depend not just on our personal deeds, but also on the health of the systems of which we are a part. These systems cannot be healed without divine intervention, without the Revelation of Bahá'u'lláh. The essence of this intervention is that we must realize that we—all of humanity—are now one. We are connected in a way that cannot be undone. Until we acknowledge our fundamental unity, all of our lives will be precarious. Revealing the holy, the sacred, aspects of this oneness is the work of the Bahá'í Faith.

In sum, then, the goal of the Bahá'í Faith is to fulfill the Lord's prayer: "Thy Kingdom come, on earth as it is in heaven." The closing paragraph of a prayer many Bahá'ís say everyday reads: "The kingdom of earth and heaven are Thine, O Lord of the worlds."[11] The prayer acknowledges that the victory is already won in the eyes of God. God has established His kingdom on earth. Humankind, however, is still in the process of discovering it.

The Creative Word

In John 16, Jesus mentioned that a Comforter would arrive to show us things to come:

> Nevertheless, I tell you the truth: It is expedient for you that I go away; *for if I go not away, the Comforter will not come unto you*; but if I depart, I will send him unto you. And when he is come he will reprove the world of sin, and righteousness, and of judgement; Of sin, because they believe not on me; Of righteousness, because I go to my father, and ye see me no more; Of judgement, because the prince of this world is judged. I have yet many things to say unto you, but ye cannot bear them now. Nevertheless, when he, the Spirit of truth, is come, he will guide you into all truth; for he shall not speak of himself, but whatever he shall hear, that shall he speak; *and he will show you things to come. John 16:7-13* (Emphasis mine.)

11. From "The Long Obligatory Prayer."

What if the Comforter does not refer to the Holy Spirit as many Christians believe, but to the Promised One? He then truly would be a Comforter and the Spirit of Truth, capable of showing us things to come. To ignore this possibility is to ignore too much.

The words of a Manifestation of God are not like those of men. His are words which create things. Bahá'u'lláh writes, "Every word that proceedeth out of the mouth of God is endowed with such potency as can instill new life into every human frame, if ye be of them that comprehend this truth."[12] However, these words apparently go far beyond regenerating human spirituality. Bahá'u'lláh continues His explanation:

> All the wondrous works ye behold in this world have been manifested through the operation of His supreme and most exalted Will, His wondrous and inflexible Purpose. *Through the mere revelation of the word "Fashioner,"* issuing forth from His lips and proclaiming this attribute to mankind, *such power is released as can regenerate, through successive ages, all the manifold arts which the hands of man can produce*. This verily is a certain truth. No sooner is the resplendent word uttered, than its animating energies, stirring within all created things, give birth to the means and instruments whereby such arts can be produced and perfected. *All the wondrous*

12. *Gleanings from the Writings of Bahá'u'lláh*, pp. 141-42.

> *achievements ye now witness are the direct consequence of the Revelation of this Name.* *Gleanings from the Writings of Bahá'u'lláh*, pp. 141-42. (Emphasis mine.)

Therefore, if they are created in an attitude of prayer and celebration, the arts are a product of Revelation. All the wondrous messianic music produced as the Revelation of Bahá'u'lláh dawned was not accidental. Handel's *Messiah* was composed in 1742. *The Battle Hymn of the Republic*, which contains the words "Mine eyes have seen the glory of the coming of the Lord," was written as Bahá'u'lláh's ministry approached. All the arts and music that are to come—once humankind discovers its Beloved—likewise will be glorious.

Beyond this, however, is another great truth of the creative word. Bahá'u'lláh continues:

> *In days to come, ye will, verily, behold things of which ye have never heard before.* Thus hath it been decreed in the Tablets of God and none can comprehend it except them whose sight is sharp. In like manner, the moment the word expressing My attribute "The Omniscient" issueth forth from My mouth, every created thing will, according to its capacity and limitations, be invested with the power *to unfold the knowledge of the most marvelous sciences*, and will be empowered to manifest

> them in the course of time at the bidding of Him Who is the Almighty, the All-Knowing.
> *Gleanings from the Writings of Bahá'u'lláh*, p. 142. (Emphasis mine.)

Recall the words of Jesus, "He will show you things to come." Have the sciences changed since the creative word of Bahá'u'lláh went forth in the middle of the nineteenth century? The answer is obvious. But now the reason for the advance of science is clear. The tools of science are to be used to accomplish God's Will, which is to establish the oneness of humankind. All the advances in transportation, electronics, physics, telecommunication, publishing, and news distribution have but one end: to supply the means for establishing the unity of the human race.

The Principles of Our Age

It is sometimes said that the Bahá'í Faith has twelve principles. It is no accident that these principles have become the defining causes of our day. They are the truth now facing us. From the moment Bahá'u'lláh affirmed them, all humankind was given the task of realizing them and the potential to do so. The principles follow:[13]

13. These principles are adapted from 'Abdu'l-Bahá, *Foundations of World Unity*, pp. 28-31.

(1) Each person bears responsibility for investigating truth independently so that humanity might be spared the consequences of blind imitation;
(2) Humanity represents an essential unity, and all people are subjects of the same God;
(3) The purpose of religion is to foster the spirit of fellowship and love; religious differences should not be made the cause of estrangement and war;
(4) Religious, racial, political, economic, and patriotic prejudices must be eliminated;
(5) An international auxiliary language must be established;
(6) The equality of men and women must be realized;
(7) Poverty must be eliminated, both through voluntary giving and through a responsibility mandated to the community;
(8) Through the Ideal Power, people must free themselves from the captivity of the world of nature which keeps them struggling for existence;
(9) We must recognize the common source of all revealed religions and know that: "Religion is, verily, the chief instrument for the establishment of order in the world, and of tranquility amongst its peoples"[14];
(10) We must understand the essential harmony of religion and science; and thus we must temper material with spiritual civilization, while we fight superstition with science;

14. Bahá'u'lláh, *Epistle to the Son of the Wolf*, p. 28.

(11) Universal education must be provided for all children;
(12) Justice must be established in the world.

This is my summary of the points made by Bahá'u'lláh, not His words (except where quoted). Other books are available which present these principles in greater detail.[15]

Which New World Order?

Perhaps one of the most exciting elements of our age is the slow emergence of a world commonwealth. Shoghi Effendi writes of this process as disclosed in the vision of Bahá'u'lláh:

> The unity of the human race, as envisioned by Bahá'u'lláh, implies the establishment of a world commonwealth in which all nations, races, creeds and classes are closely and permanently united, and in which the autonomy of its state members and the personal freedom and initiative of the individuals that compose them are definitely and completely safeguarded. This commonwealth must, as far as we

15. See John Ferraby, *All Things Made New: A Comprehensive Outline of the Bahá'í Faith* (London: Bahá'í Publishing Trust, 1975) and J.E. Esselmont, *Bahá'u'lláh and the New Era: An Introduction to the Bahá'í Faith* (Wilmette, Illinois: Bahá'í Publishing Trust, 1970).

can visualize it, consist of a world legislature, whose members will, as the trustees of the whole of mankind, ultimately control the entire resources of all the component nations, and will enact such laws as shall be required to regulate life, satisfy the needs and adjust the relationships of all races and peoples. A world executive, backed by an international Force, will carry out the decisions arrived at, and apply the laws enacted by, this world legislature, and will safeguard the organic unity of the world commonwealth. A world tribunal will adjudicate and deliver its compulsory and final verdict in all and any disputes that may arise between the various elements constituting this universal system . . .[16]

The nations of the world have taken several steps toward this goal, the first was with the establishment of the League of Nations (1914), and the second was the formation of the United Nations (1945). The League of Nations failed and was replaced by the United Nations, which has often been frustrated by the politics of a deeply divided world. With the end of the Cold War, the United Nations may be able to find a true unity and move closer, in spirit, to the institution envisioned by Bahá'u'lláh. But this new unity must be a solemn spiritual unity.

Bahá'ís, of course, are busy building their own world order, according to the directives of Bahá'u'lláh. Certainly, they cooperate with any person, institution, or

16. Shoghi Effendi, *The World Order of Bahá'u'lláh*, p. 203.

government engaged in the pursuit of the oneness of humanity, but they also have their own system. Bahá'í communities operate on three levels of organization: local, national, and international. The supervising and directing institutions of these levels are referred to respectively as Local Spiritual Assemblies, National Spiritual Assemblies, and the Universal House of Justice. Each of these institutions is freely elected in a nonpolitical process. That is, no one runs for office, no campaigning is allowed, no money changes hands, no constituencies are served, and all adults are eligible for local and national service. The terms of service are limited and the service is generally uncompensated. No single elected member has any more power or authority than any other single believer. Only the Assemblies or the House of Justice have more authority than individuals and the scope of this authority has been limited by Bahá'u'lláh, Who has also set up an appeals system. More detailed accounts of how Bahá'í communities operate can be found in other sources.[17]

Recently, books have appeared which attack the idea of a new world order. I am thinking especially of Pat Robertson's *The New World Order.*[18] He attacks an emerging world order led by a secret society of cultural elitists who are inspired by the occult.[19] This elite, is

17. See Shoghi Effendi, *The World Order of Bahá'u'lláh* and also *Bahá'í Administration* by the same author.

18. USA: Successful Living Edition, 1991.

19. Robertson inexplicably traces the occult influence to Adam Weishaupt and his Order of the Illuminati formed on May 1, 1776. According to Robertson, this small secret society not only gained

comprised of "the internationalists, the banking and industrial complex, the European socialists, and their allies" . . . "seeking global control of the world's money, natural resources, and military power so that they can establish themselves, whether the people like it or not, as the dominant elite to determine the type of world we all will live in."[20] Robertson characterizes the goals of this new world order this way:

> As I have pointed out, the common strain that permeates much of the thinking about a new world order involves four basic premises: (1) the elimination of private property, (2) the elimination of national governments and national sovereignty, (3) the elimination of traditional Judeo-Christian theism, and (4) a world government controlled by an elite made up of those who are considered to be superior, or in the occultic sense, "adepts" or "illuminated."[21]

Contrary to what Robertson claims, this would not be a new world order. It would be the old world order

control of European Freemasons and ultimately caused the French Revolution, but also inspired the Communist Manifesto. Through communism a plan was devised to seemingly liberalize Europe (and the Soviet Union) and lull the West into forming closer ties with a communist system which would eventually degenerate in favor of a world unity led by the Illuminati, whose driving force was satanic ambition and the lust for power.

20. Robertson, *The New World Order*, p. 33.
21. Robertson, *The New World Order*, p. 71.

grown to international dimension. There have always been those who wanted to take the money of others, subjugate governments for their own interests, eliminate irritating religions, and adorn themselves with the mantle of intellectual superiority. The old order which Robertson supposes to be the Christian world order, has never existed. Dare we call any order of the past truly Christian?

What is Christian is the promise of a new world. It will not be the one that Robertson justly condemns. However, it also will not be one that comes down from the clouds. It will be one that people build with the realization that the Promised Day has come and that we are accountable to respond. This new world order is distinctly international. (It would have to be in order for it to be a *world* order.) In this new world order America will have a prominent place, but it will not have the central place. We too must think about what it means to live as but one nation under the fatherhood of God. We too must be prepared to be reprimanded when we do wrong and praised when we do right.

In this new world order of Bahá'u'lláh, private property has been safeguarded. Communism and excessive centralization have been expressly condemned. The sovereignty of nations has been protected. Indeed, Bahá'u'lláh makes His subjects conform to the laws of whatever government they fall under, and they are encouraged to pray for and assist the government in whatever way they can. And of course, the Bahá'í Faith claims to be the fulfillment of the Judeo-Christian tradition. Finally, there are no self-appointed cultural or intellectual elites with special powers in the Bahá'í system. There is no secret society. And there is no clergy.

It is not just the force of history that pushes us toward a global system; it is the hand of God. It is doubtlessly true that many of the decision-makers of our times have been corrupted by an earthly lust for power. But these people, motivated by whatever force, cannot stand, and will not get in the way of God fulfilling His purpose. We will have a world government and a world economy, but it will eventually be subservient to that greater Kingdom which is God's.

Chapter 15

THE APOCALYPSE

We are, all of us, very busy these days. Materialists and religious advocates both are consumed by their quests. I fear that the materialists are so occupied with securing their positions in our secular Babylon that they will not take time to consider a Prophet's call. And I fear that those who deem themselves religious are so busy defending their current religious views that they may fail to consider the claims of the very One Who determines if these views are correct. These signs do not augur well for the future.

Both the Bible and Bahá'í writings tell us that darkness will envelop us after the coming of the Promised One.[1] The darkness has now fallen. It is only our future which will be glorious. The Bible promises that God, "has remembered our iniquities."[2] As a consequence, we have been promised seven bowls of wrath. We in Babylon, and those who make up the beast, have not yet repented. The earth is filled with horrible sights, and the

1. "Immediately after the tribulation of those days [of the coming of the Son of man] shall the sun be darkened, and the moon shall not give its light, and the stars shall fall from heaven, and the powers of the earth shall be shaken." *Matthew 24:29.*

2. *Revelation 18:5.*

old heavens of guidance do not aid us because we have not set our sight on the new Light. The times, therefore, are perilous. Bahá'u'lláh writes:

> O ye peoples of the world! Know, verily, that an unforeseen calamity is following you, and that grievous retribution awaiteth you. Think not the deeds ye have committed have been blotted from My sight. By My beauty! All your doings hath My Pen graven with open characters upon tablets of chrysolite. *Gleanings from the Writings of Bahá'u'lláh*, p. 209-210.

Babylon is falling, and we are living in it. The beast is raging against the Promised One, and we are uncommitted. The truth of our times is that, once the call of the Promised One is heard, there are only three sides to choose from: the beast, Babylon, and the Promised One. With which will we side?

If we could see clearly, we would recognize that we are in the midst of judgment. Before our eyes, the old world order is being rolled up and a new one laid out in its stead. Bahá'u'lláh advises:

> Beseech ye the one true God to grant that all men may be graciously assisted to fulfil that which is acceptable in Our sight. Soon will the

> present-day order be rolled up, and a new one spread out in its stead. Verily, thy Lord speaketh the truth, and is the Knower of things unseen. *Gleanings from the Writings of Bahá'u'lláh*, p. 7.

The calamities that are occurring around us are ample testimony to the deficiencies of our old world order. These tribulations are themselves the proof that we must abandon the old ways. We need a new heaven and a new earth, a new system of guidance and a new order. Will we abandon our old ways before greater calamities fall? The question is left open in Bahá'í writings.

It is not easy to join a new religion. In the countries of the East, it often has meant the possibility of sacrificing one's life. In the countries of the West, it has meant becoming a target for ridicule and a subject of controversy. In both places Bahá'ís have been confronted with ridiculous arguments, often contentious even within mainstream Judaic, Christian, or Islamic thought. When pamphlets are written attacking the Bahá'í Faith, it is common for both sides to be misrepresented. In these works there is no fairness at all. There is no academic competency, nor even decency. Bahá'ís suffer in quiet the curse of the fanatic. They are made to carry the cross others make for them. Yet, the ambition of the accuser will ultimately be revealed.

It takes courage to become a Bahá'í. Once it took courage to become a Christian or a Muslim. I have made my decision, and I have laid out some of my reasoning in this book. As I said at the start, these reasons are necessarily incomplete. What makes faith whole is not prophecy but existential contact with the grace of the Beloved. It is this grace which the Bible said is the Promised One's reward. The verses read: "And behold, I come quickly, and my reward is with me, to give to every man according as his work shall be." (Revelation 22:12.) With this great Revelation before us, how shall our work be? How will we respond?

Appendix

THOUGHTS ON THE SEVEN SEALS

The warning to the seven churches is the first major topic in the Book of Revelation. The second is the throne-room scene in heaven. In this scene there is a central throne surrounded by twenty-four smaller thrones on which the elders sit.[1] Before the central throne are four fantastic creatures who continually sing the praises of God. The One on the central throne has a scroll sealed with seven seals. A Lamb, also called a Lion from the tribe of Judah (whom I take to be Jesus), has been slain and won the right to open the seals. He opens them one at a time. As mentioned in the text above, Bahá'í's have no authoritative commentary on this scene. It is possible, however, to suggest some meanings that are consistent with other commentary made by the Central Figures of the Bahá'í Faith.

1. The twenty-four elders are not identified in scripture. Traditionally, they are interpreted as referring to a symbolic unity of Old and New Testaments, i.e., twelve tribes and twelve apostles.

The Four Horsemen

The set of seven seals is divided into a set of four and a set of three. As the first four seals are broken, the four horsemen of the apocalypse issue forth. The horse of the first rider is white, the same color as the horse that the Promised One rides (Chapter 19). The rider of the first horse of the apocalypse, however, is obviously not the Promised One. He goes forth with bow and crown "conquering and to conquer." He brings war and conflict and there is no evidence of salvation or justice in his work. His is a military endeavor. Christian interpreters have often called this rider a false christ, as he assumes the position of the Promised One on a white horse. I think this is close to correct. However, the horseman more properly represents those who advance their selfish interests through military means in the guise of religion. Further, as Jesus unlocked the seals, we have first to recall the most obvious examples of Christian history: the conquering that was done in the name of Christ, but that was not Christian. The Inquisitions; numerous European religious wars; the virtual annihilation of large portions of the original populations of South and North America as well as numerous island peoples; the enslavement of Africa, India, and much of China; and the Holocaust.

The second horseman brought war; the third, famine; and the fourth, death. All of these may be seen as the consequences of the European ("Christian") national movements that are so prominent in history. And true to the proportions of these historic movements, the verses tell us that death was given power "over the fourth part of the earth."

An alternative, though I think weaker, interpretation of the four horsemen is that they symbolize the general destruction which humanity has brought on itself, not necessarily related to a misdirected Christianity.

As with the wars, famines, pestilence, earthquakes, and false prophets of Matthew 24, the signs of the four horsemen, however interpreted, may be seen as the continuing background upon which other prophetic actions occur.

The Later Seals: General Approach

The fifth, sixth, and seventh seal are more difficult to interpret. The interpretation is made more complex by the presence of a lengthy interlude between the opening of the sixth and seventh seals, which many have supposed is misplaced text. Two interpretations suggest themselves from a Bahá'í perspective: The fifth, sixth, and seventh seal, together with the interlude, may relate to Islam; or, the fifth seal only may relate to Islam, while the sixth relates to the Revelation of the Báb, and the seventh to that of Bahá'u'lláh. I favor the first interpretation.

The Last Three Seals as Islamic

When the fifth seal is opened, we are told, a company of new believers will be killed for their faith and added to those previously slain.[2] It makes sense to think of these believers as Muslim for several reasons. The chief reason is that the Christian martyrs are already under the alter of God. Also, as with the martyrdom of early Christians, the martyrdom of early Muslims took place under similar circumstances: Both were victims of very much more powerful groups. As Christianity and Islam grew in strength, the conflicts which arose between these religions and other groups were often confounded with national interests. The Christians and Muslims that were killed in these later times may have been killed not so much because of their religion, but because they were seen as agents of a foreign national power intent upon conquering the weaker countries. Under these conditions, it is difficult to regard the later Christians and later Muslims as always innocent and pure victims of religious persecution. Thus, those who are under the alter of God as the fifth seal is broken are probably early Christians, and those who are yet to be killed are early Muslims.

As the sixth seal is broken, there is an earthquake, the stars fall, the sun turns black, the kings of the earth

2. "And when he had opened the fifth seal, I saw under the altar the souls of them that were slain for the word of God, and for the testimony which they held: And they cried with a loud voice, saying, How long, O Lord, holy and true, dost thou not judge and avenge our blood on them that dwell on the earth? And white robes were given unto every one of them; and it was said unto them, that they should rest yet for a little season, *until their fellow servants also and their brethren, that should be killed as they were,* should be fulfilled." *Revelation 6:9-11* (Emphasis mine.)

hide.[3] The earthquake represents the shaking of the foundations of a society, the stars are leaders who fall, the sun is the light a society turns to, and the kings who hide are those who eventually have to face the consequences of their disbelief. These symbols are explained in greater detail by Bahá'u'lláh in *The Kitáb-i-Íqán*. While this may be an end-time prophecy, the images may apply to the coming of any Prophet of God, including Muḥammad.

The interlude between the sixth and seventh seal allows more detail to be added to the ministry of Islam. The time for the judgment of the entire world has not yet come. As the verses inform us, the four angels holding the winds of God's wrath are being restrained.[4] The angel who comes from the East, with the seal of the living God, is Muḥammad—the Seal of the Prophets. His

3. "And I beheld when he had opened the sixth seal, and, lo, there was a great earthquake; and the sun became black as sackcloth of hair, and the moon became as blood; And the stars of heaven fell unto the earth, even as a fig tree casteth her untimely figs, when she is shaken of a mighty wind. And the heaven departed as a scroll when it is rolled together; and every mountain and island were moved out of their places. And the kings of the earth, and the great men, and the rich men, and the chief captains, and the mighty men, and every bondman, and every free man, hid themselves in the dens and in the rocks of the mountains; And said to the mountains and rocks, Fall on us, and hide us from the face of him that sitteth on the throne, and from the wrath of the Lamb: For the great day of his wrath is come; and who shall be able to stand." *Revelation 6:12-17*

4. The interlude begins, "And after these things I saw four angels standing on the four corners of the earth, holding the four

followers are still in the East when compared to the followers of Christ, who are in the West. And, His ministry accomplished just what the verses say: He sealed (tested) the faith of Jews and Christians. One hundred and forty-four thousand Jews were sealed. The large number is merely symbolic of completeness, and of a return of Jews to Israel at the end of the dispensation of Islam. The great multitude of Christians that appears in the interlude, those purified by the blood of the Lamb, would also be sealed.[5] They pass through the dispensation of Islam and appear victorious awaiting the Promised One, as the dispensation ends.

Finally, the seventh seal is opened. There is silence for awhile, and then the seven angels who stand before God are given trumpets.[6] The opening of the seventh seal brings us to the beginning of the Bahá'í era in 1844.

winds of the earth, that the wind should not blow on the earth, nor on the sea, nor on any tree. And I saw another angel ascending from the east, having the seal of the living God; and he cried with a loud voice to the four angels, to whom it was given to hurt the earth and the sea. Saying, Hurt not the earth neither the sea, nor the trees, till we have sealed the servants of our God in their foreheads." *Revelation 7:1-3*

5. "After this I beheld and, lo, a great multitude, which no man could number, of all nations, and kindreds, and peoples, and tongues, stood before the throne, and before the Lamb, clothed with white robes, and palms in their hands. And cried with a loud voice, saying, Salvation to our God who sitteth upon the throne, and unto the Lamb." *Revelation 7:9-10*

6. "And when he had opened the seventh seal, there was silence in heaven about the space of half an hour. And I saw the seven angels who stood before God, and to them were given seven trumpets." *Revelation 8:1-2*

There is silence for awhile because Bahá'u'lláh does not, at first, appear. It is His forerunner, the Báb, who appears first. The verses state that another angel appears at the alter before God.[7] This would be the Báb, at the alter of sacrifice. Again we have the signs of a new Revelation: an earthquake of faith and storms of controversy and opposition. Humankind is condemned in its response. The result is the destruction of the first four trumpet blasts. The fifth, sixth, and seventh trumpet blasts retell the story of Islam, the episode of the Báb, and the appearance of the Promised One, Bahá'u'lláh—adding detail.

The second interpretation, where the fifth event in the series above refers to Islam, the sixth event to the Bábí Faith, and the seventh to the Bahá'í Faith, can be made with minor modifications to what is above.

7. "And another angel came and stood at the altar, having a golden censer; and there was given unto him much incense, that he should offer it with the prayers of all saints upon the golden altar which was before the throne. And the smoke of the incense, which came with the prayers of the saints, ascended up before God out of the angel's hand. And the angel took the censer, and filled it with fire from the altar, and cast it upon the earth; and there were voices, and thunderclaps, and lightnings, and an earthquake. And the seven angels who had the seven trumpets prepared themselves to sound." *Revelation 8:3-6.*

+183 Carmel & Sharon

√197 All nations to mnt of God.

√ 189,90 Humble before kings
(not Most Great Peace First)

√121-124 all nations - several quotes

√232 UN. LofNs.

√234 vs Robertson's negative vision of world order

INDEX TO BIBLICAL REFERENCES